• CLASSIC AMERICAN FURNITURE SERIES •

# NORTHWOODS FURNITURE

JIM STACK

**POPULAR WOODWORKING BOOKS**
CINCINNATI, OHIO

www.popularwoodworking.com

## READ THIS IMPORTANT SAFETY NOTICE

To prevent accidents, keep safety in mind while you work. Use the safety guards installed on power equipment; they are for your protection. When working on power equipment, keep fingers away from saw blades, wear safety goggles to prevent injuries from flying wood chips and sawdust, wear headphones to protect your hearing, and consider installing a dust vacuum to reduce the amount of airborne sawdust in your woodshop. Don't wear loose clothing, such as neckties or shirts with loose sleeves, or jewelry, such as rings, necklaces or bracelets, when working on power equipment. Tie back long hair to prevent it from getting caught in your equipment. People who are sensitive to certain chemicals should check the chemical content of any product before using it. The author and editors who compiled this book have tried to make the contents as accurate and correct as possible. Plans, illustrations, photographs and text have been carefully checked. All instructions, plans and projects should be carefully read, studied and understood before beginning construction. Due to the variability of local conditions, construction materials, skill levels, etc., neither the author nor Popular Woodworking Books assumes any responsibility for any accidents, injuries, damages or other losses incurred resulting from the material presented in this book.

## METRIC CONVERSION CHART

| TO CONVERT | TO | MULTIPLY BY |
|---|---|---|
| Inches | Centimeters | 2.54 |
| Centimeters | Inches | 0.4 |
| Feet | Centimeters | 30.5 |
| Centimeters | Feet | 0.03 |
| Yards | Meters | 0.9 |
| Meters | Yards | 1.1 |
| Sq. Inches | Sq. Centimeters | 6.45 |
| Sq. Centimeters | Sq. Inches | 0.16 |
| Sq. Feet | Sq. Meters | 0.09 |
| Sq. Meters | Sq. Feet | 10.8 |
| Sq. Yards | Sq. Meters | 0.8 |
| Sq. Meters | Sq. Yards | 1.2 |
| Pounds | Kilograms | 0.45 |
| Kilograms | Pounds | 2.2 |
| Ounces | Grams | 28.4 |
| Grams | Ounces | 0.04 |

Visit our Web site at www.popularwoodworking.com for information on more resources for woodworkers.

Other fine Popular Woodworking Books are available from your local bookstore or direct from the publisher.

05   04   03   02   01      5   4   3   2   1

**Library of Congress Cataloging-in-Publication Data**

Stack, Jim
   Northwoods furniture / [by Jim Stack].--[1st ed.].
     p. cm.
   Includes index.
   ISBN 1-55870-569-4 (alk. paper)
   1. Furniture making--Amateurs' manuals. 2. Country furniture--Amateurs' manuals. 3. Rustic woodwork--Amateurs' manuals. I. Title.

TT195 .S67 2001
684.1'04--dc21                                                     2001021007

Edited by Jennifer Churchill
Content edited by Michael Berger
Designed by Brian Roeth
Page layout by Patrick J. McCarthy
Production coordinated by Emily Gross
Finished projects and cover photographed by Christine Polomsky
Step-by-step photography by Jim Stack
Computer illustrations by Melanie Powell, Studio in the Woods/Illustration for the Technically Inclined, 2202 Deer Trail Rd., Coopersburg, PA 18036, 215-538-2237, mjp1@fast.net.

Jim Stack is a cabinetmaker/furniture maker with more than 22 years of building experience in commercial cabinet shops. He also had his own business for 5½ years during which time he designed and built custom cabinets and furniture. He has taught woodworking classes at a local hardwood retailer and feels that this experience helped him learn how to communicate effectively as a woodworking instructor. He is currently the acquisitions editor for Popular Woodworking Books. Jim has made and continues to make lots of mistakes, which he feels is the best way to learn. (Although, of course, he doesn't make these mistakes on purpose!) He also feels that woodworking should be fun and rewarding for the builder. His advice is to make your plans carefully, start making sawdust and have fun!

*about the author*

**DEDICATION**
*This book is dedicated to my parents: To my mother, for encouraging me to be curious about everything, and to my father, for allowing me to make lots of sawdust and noise in his woodshop.*

*acknowledgements*

I would like to thank Julie and Tom Stinchcomb for letting us invade their gorgeous log home and have the run of the place while photographing all the projects in this book. Thank you!

Many thanks to Jenny Ziegler for helping create the branch furniture. She is a joy to work with!

I thank my editor, friend and co-worker Jennifer Churchill for helping me properly say what I wanted to say, what I needed to say and to say it when it needed to be said!

And to the rest of the team — photographer Christine Polomsky, book designer Brian Roeth and photo stylist Sharon Sweeney — who all made the photo shoot for this book a lot of fun. It was a great team effort!

# introduction

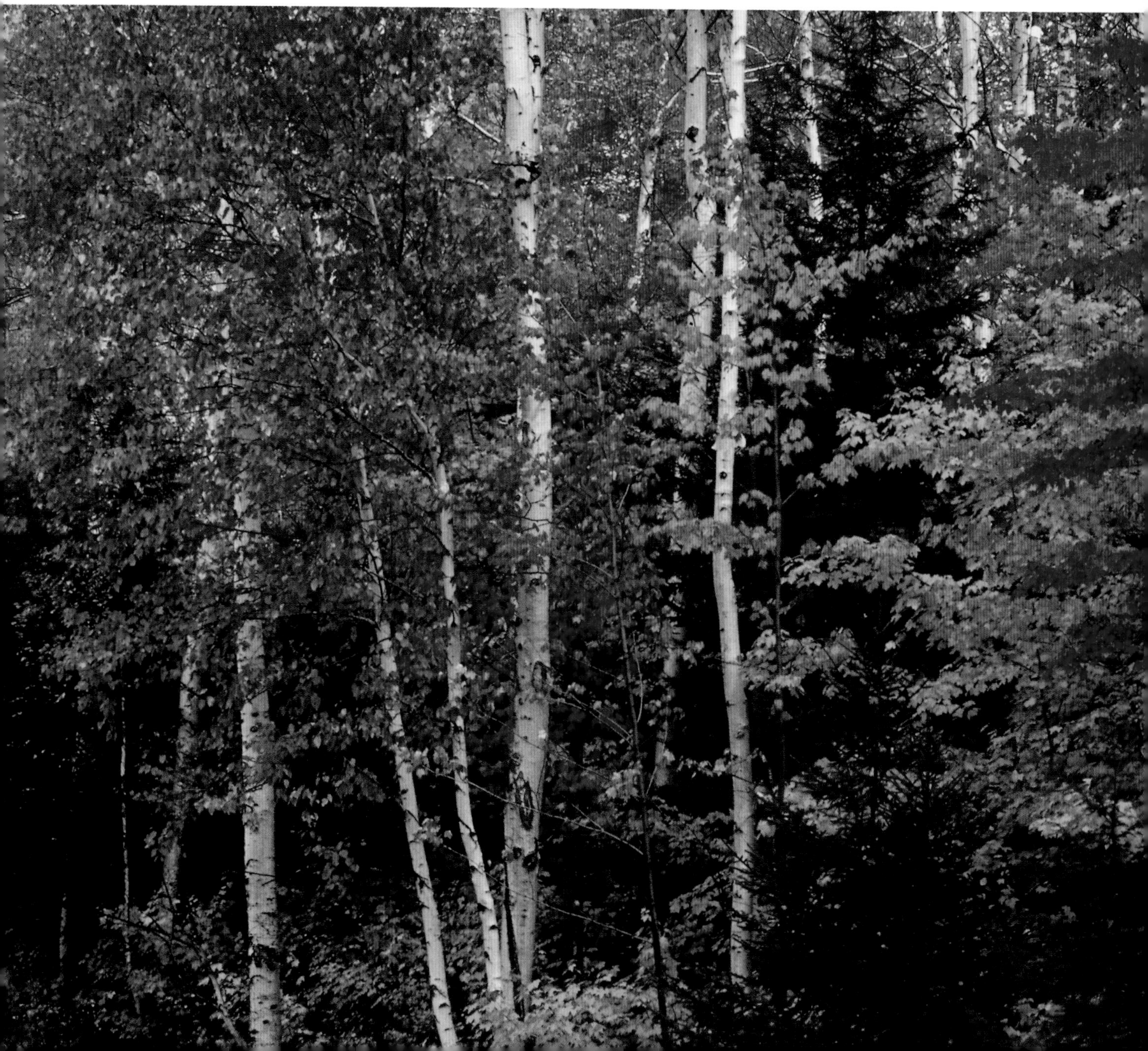

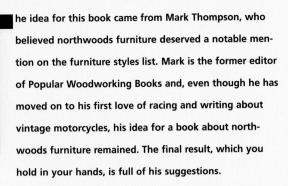

**T**he idea for this book came from Mark Thompson, who believed northwoods furniture deserved a notable mention on the furniture styles list. Mark is the former editor of Popular Woodworking Books and, even though he has moved on to his first love of racing and writing about vintage motorcycles, his idea for a book about northwoods furniture remained. The final result, which you hold in your hands, is full of his suggestions.

When I started doing research for this book, I discovered a huge following of people who love rustic furniture. The list included collectors, antique dealers, folks with get-away-from-it-all cabins (how I wish I was in that group!), restaurant owners and auto mechanics. In short, all kinds of people from all walks of life.

I think the strong interest (or, in some cases, downright fanaticism) stems from the images evoked by this type of furniture: a cozy cabin on a lake or in the woods, a fire in the fireplace, hot stew on the stove and a game of chess in progress ... you know, images that evoke those basic, warm-fuzzy feelings.

Most of us have an idea of what rustic means: woodsy, well-used, comfortable. The furniture in this book is functional with a solid, new look yet it still captures that well-worn aesthetic. These projects begin with basic log cabin (or lodge) furniture styles, which are then transformed into comfortable pieces of furniture, for a cozy-cabin addition to any room.

Building this furniture is fun and rewarding. Once the tools are quiet and the dust has settled, it's very satisfying to just stand back and look at the work you've done and admire the furniture that has taken shape. That's why woodworkers do what they do.

Using basic woodshop tools and time-tested construction techniques — like mortise-and-tenon, frame-and-panel, and the more recent method of biscuit joinery — the home woodworker can create classic northwoods furniture that will last for generations.

# rough-sawn pine bed

AFTER A HARD DAY OF CHOPPING wood, hiking or fishing, having a place to rest your weary bones is essential. This queen-size bed allows plenty of room to stretch out. The side rails are attached with bolts to the head- and footboards, making this an extremely sturdy bed. Two more perks: The footboard is just the right height to throw your clothes onto, and the bed has enough height off the floor to stow your boots under it.

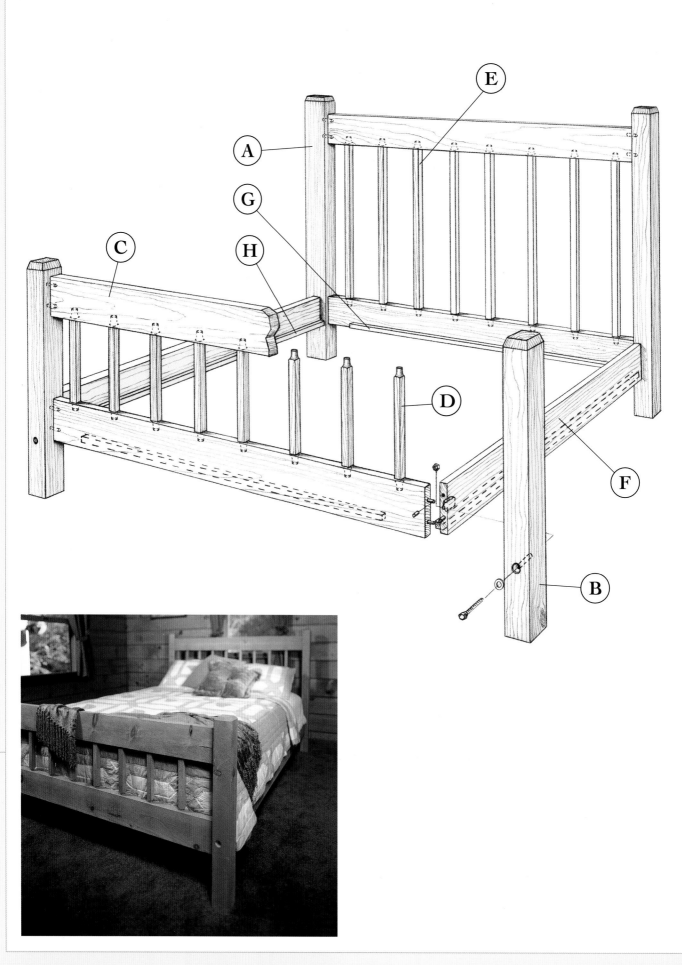

**MATERIALS LIST (INCHES)** • ROUGH–SAWN PINE BED

| REF. | QTY. | PART | MATERIAL | THICKNESS | WIDTH | LENGTH | COMMENTS |
|------|------|------|----------|-----------|-------|--------|----------|
| A | 2 | Legs | Sugar Pine | 3 | 3 | 47 | |
| B | 2 | Legs | Sugar Pine | 3 | 3 | 30 | |
| C | 4 | Rails | Sugar Pine | 1⅜ | 5½ | 59¼ | |
| D | 8 | Spindles | Sugar Pine | 1 | 1 | 11 | 1" tenons on each end |
| E | 8 | Spindles | Sugar Pine | 1 | 1 | 27½ | 1" tenons on each end |
| F | 2 | Side Rails | Sugar Pine | 1⅜ | 5½ | 79¼ | |
| G | 2 | Cleats | Sugar Pine | 1¼ | 1¼ | 48 | |
| H | 2 | Cleats | Sugar Pine | 1¼ | 1¼ | 79 | |
| | 4 | ⅜" x 6" Bolt | | | | | |
| | 8 | ⅜" Flat Washers | | | | | |
| | 4 | ⅜" Nuts | | | | | |
| | 8 | ½" x 2" Gluing Dowels | | | | | |

Note: This bed is for a queen-size mattress (60"-wide by 80"-long).

**MATERIALS LIST (MILLIMETERS)** • ROUGH–SAWN PINE BED

| REF. | QTY. | PART | MATERIAL | THICKNESS | WIDTH | LENGTH | COMMENTS |
|------|------|------|----------|-----------|-------|--------|----------|
| A | 2 | Legs | Sugar Pine | 75 | 75 | 1195 | |
| B | 2 | Legs | Sugar Pine | 75 | 75 | 765 | |
| C | 4 | Rails | Sugar Pine | 35 | 140 | 1505 | |
| D | 8 | Spindles | Sugar Pine | 25 | 25 | 280 | 25mm tenons on each end |
| E | 8 | Spindles | Sugar Pine | 25 | 25 | 700 | 25mm tenons on each end |
| F | 2 | Side Rails | Sugar Pine | 35 | 140 | 2015 | |
| G | 2 | Cleats | Sugar Pine | 32 | 32 | 1220 | |
| H | 2 | Cleats | Sugar Pine | 32 | 32 | 2000 | |
| | 4 | 9.5mm x 150mm Bolt | | | | | |
| | 8 | 9.5mm Flat Washers | | | | | |
| | 4 | 9.5mm Nuts | | | | | |
| | 8 | 12mm x 50mm Gluing Dowels | | | | | |

1 | Use a ⅝" (16mm) tenon cutter to create tenons on all the spindles. This tool (called a power tenon cutter and made by Veritas) is available from Lee Valley Tools. You will find it invaluable when making the branch furniture.

*Standard Bed Sizes in/mm*

| STANDARD NAME | WIDTH | LENGTH |
|---|---|---|
| Twin | 39/990 | 75/1,905 |
| Double or Full | 54/1,370 | 75/1,905 |
| Queen | 60/1,525 | 80/2,030 |
| King | 76/1,930 | 80/2,030 |
| California King | 72/1,830 | 84/2,135 |

2 | By laying out the four rails together, it is easy to mark all the tenon holes on all rails at one time, ensuring that they will line up. This also ensures that the spindles will be square to the rails at final assembly.

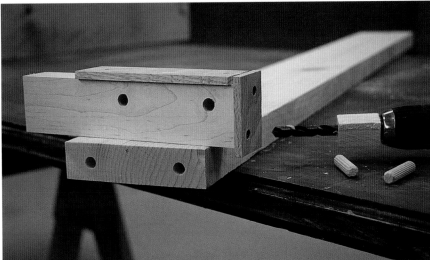

3 | Use a homemade doweling jig to drill the dowel holes in the ends of the side rails. (See sidebar "Making a Homemade Doweling Jig" on page 14.)

4 | Use the same jig for drilling all the dowel holes needed to assemble the headboard and footboard. Note the use of different fences and stops on the jig. This makes one jig very versatile.

5 | Cutting the bevels on the ends of the four corner posts is done easily on the table saw. Tilt the saw blade to 45°, and use the miter gauge to hold the posts. (Note the use of a stop block to register the end of the post to the saw blade.) Simply "roll" the post to make each cut.

6 | Glue up and assemble the headboard. By using a flat surface and putting blocks under the rails to raise the assembly, clamping is done easily.

## MAKING A HOMEMADE DOWELING JIG

When you have a specialized type of doweling application, making your own jig is the simplest way to solve the problem. Using a hard wood like rock maple or birch is best. Minimum thickness should be 1".
Use a drill press to make the guide holes, so they will come out clean and straight. Then cut angles or add stops.

**7** Use a routing jig with a square hole to cut the cavity for the washer and nut. (Double-check to be sure to rout the cavity on the inside of the rail.)

**8** The front stop-rail on the jig doubles as a hole-drilling block like a doweling jig. (This jig is simply clamped in place, the cavity is routed, then the bolt hole is drilled. It takes about 2 minutes for this whole procedure.)

**9** This detail shows the setup for attaching the side rails to the headboard and footboard. Though this is a queen-size bed — larger than most cabin beds — the comfort gained is worth the sacrifice of lost space! If space is limited, see the chart on page 12 and scale your bed accordingly. The spindles in the headboard and footboard add a visual lightness to the bed (and they make good handles when you need to move the bed).

# boot storage bench

THIS BENCH IS MORE THAN JUST A place to sit down and take off your boots. You can also stow your skis and poles in the rack and slide your gloves onto the rabbit-ear dryers. There's plenty of room inside the bench to store extra hiking boots, work boots or maybe a pair of snowshoes. When the lid is closed, the continuous hinge provides plenty of strength for sitting.

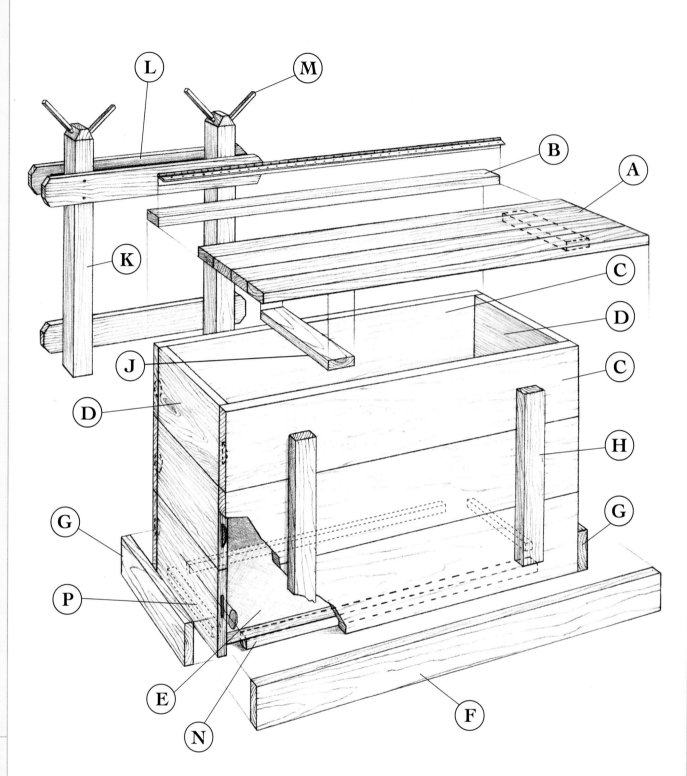

## MATERIALS LIST (INCHES) • BOOT STORAGE BENCH

| REF. | QTY. | PART | MATERIAL | THICKNESS | WIDTH | LENGTH | COMMENTS |
|------|------|------|----------|-----------|-------|--------|----------|
| A | 1 | Lid | Sugar Pine | 1 | $13^3/_8$ | 35 | |
| B | 1 | Top Rail | Sugar Pine | 1 | 2 | 35 | |
| C | 2 | Front & Back Panels | Sugar Pine | $3/_4$ | 18 | 33 | |
| D | 2 | Ends | Sugar Pine | $3/_4$ | 18 | $12^1/_2$ | |
| E | 1 | Bottom | Sugar Pine | $3/_4$ | $12^1/_2$ | $31^1/_2$ | |
| F | 1 | Base Front | Sugar Pine | $3/_4$ | 3 | $34^1/_2$ | |
| G | 2 | Base Returns | Sugar Pine | $3/_4$ | 3 | $14^1/_2$ | |
| H | 2 | Front Battens | Sugar Pine | $3/_4$ | 2 | 12 | |
| J | 2 | Inside Lid Battens | Sugar Pine | $3/_4$ | 2 | 11 | |
| K | 2 | Rack Posts | Sugar Pine | $2^1/_2$ | $2^1/_2$ | 31 | |
| L | 3 | Rack Rails | Sugar Pine | 1 | 5 | 33 | |
| M | 4 | Glove Pegs | Sugar Pine | 1 | 1 | 7 | $3/_4$" dia. x 1" tenon on one end of peg |
| N | 2 | Cleats | Sugar Pine | 1 | 1 | 29 | |
| P | 2 | Cleats | Sugar Pine | 1 | 1 | 12 | |
| | 1 | $1^1/_2$" x 35" Continuous Hinge | | | | | |

## MATERIALS LIST (MILLIMETERS) • BOOT STORAGE BENCH

| REF. | QTY. | PART | MATERIAL | THICKNESS | WIDTH | LENGTH | COMMENTS |
|------|------|------|----------|-----------|-------|--------|----------|
| A | 1 | Lid | Sugar Pine | 25 | 340 | 890 | |
| B | 1 | Top Rail | Sugar Pine | 25 | 50 | 890 | |
| C | 2 | Front & Back Panels | Sugar Pine | 19 | 460 (H) | 840 | |
| D | 2 | Ends | Sugar Pine | 19 | 460 (H) | 315 | |
| E | 1 | Bottom | Sugar Pine | 19 | 315 | 802 | |
| F | 1 | Base Front | Sugar Pine | 19 | 75 | 878 | |
| G | 2 | Base Returns | Sugar Pine | 19 | 75 | 353 | |
| H | 2 | Front Battens | Sugar Pine | 19 | 50 | 300 | |
| J | 2 | Inside Lid Battens | Sugar Pine | 19 | 50 | 280 | |
| K | 2 | Rack Posts | Sugar Pine | 65 | 65 | 790 | |
| L | 3 | Rack Rails | Sugar Pine | 25 | 130 | 840 | |
| M | 4 | Glove Pegs | Sugar Pine | 25 | 25 | 180 | 19mm dia. x 25mm tenon on one end of peg |
| N | 2 | Cleats | Sugar Pine | 25 | 25 | 735 | |
| P | 2 | Cleats | Sugar Pine | 25 | 25 | 305 | |
| | 1 | 38mm x 890mm Continuous Hinge | | | | | |

1 | Cut out all the parts as shown in the materials list. Using biscuits and glue, assemble the box first.

2 | Check for squareness before final clamping.

3 | Install cleats for attaching the bottom. These can be glued into place.

4 Drill oversize (¼") {6mm} holes in the cleats, drop the bottom panel into place and attach it with screws. These larger holes allow the screws to move with the solid wood bottom yet still hold it in place.

5 Glue the top rail in place. The continuous hinge will be screwed to this rail and the lid.

6 Cut the opposing bevels on the back posts using the table saw and a stop block attached to the miter gauge.

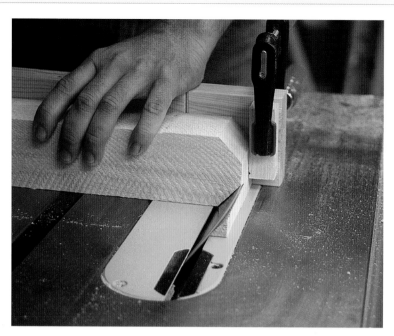

7 | Simply roll the post 180° to make the second cut.

8 | Drill oversize holes through the box sides and front, and attach the bottom moulding with screws from the inside of the box.

9 | Cut the bevels on the back slats using the table saw or chop saw. Use two spacers, as shown in the photo, to keep the posts parallel. Attach the slats to the posts with screws. Do not use any glue.

**10** Drill oversize holes in the back of the box where the posts will be located, and screw the post assembly into place from the inside of the box.

**11** Attach the continuous hinge to the lid first, then set the lid into place and screw the hinge to the top rail.

12 | To attach the lid to the box, stand the lid on the edge of the open hinge. Then the screws can be inserted.

13 | Battens are attached to the front with screws through oversize holes from the inside of the box. The battens are attached to the lid with screws through holes in the battens into the lid.

# HOW TO CREATE A ROUGH-SAWN TEXTURE

1 | Unplug the table saw and bend 5 or 6 teeth out of set by about 1/16" (alternately bend the teeth; one to the right and the next to the left).

2 | The uneven saw-blade teeth provide rough-sawn results. Remember to wear eye protection.

3 | Detail of the rough-sawn texture.

# mirror frame

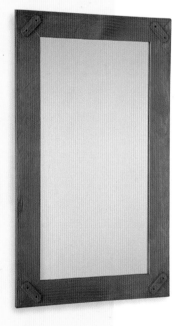

THIS IS A BASIC MIRROR OR PICTURE frame, with a couple of changes: The frame is rough-sawn, with cleats attached to the face at the corners for a more hand-hewn look and for added strength. This is a good first project; you'll get a feel for the rough-sawn cutting techniques. The frame matches the bedroom furniture in this book, but it would also look good in a hallway or in the bathroom.

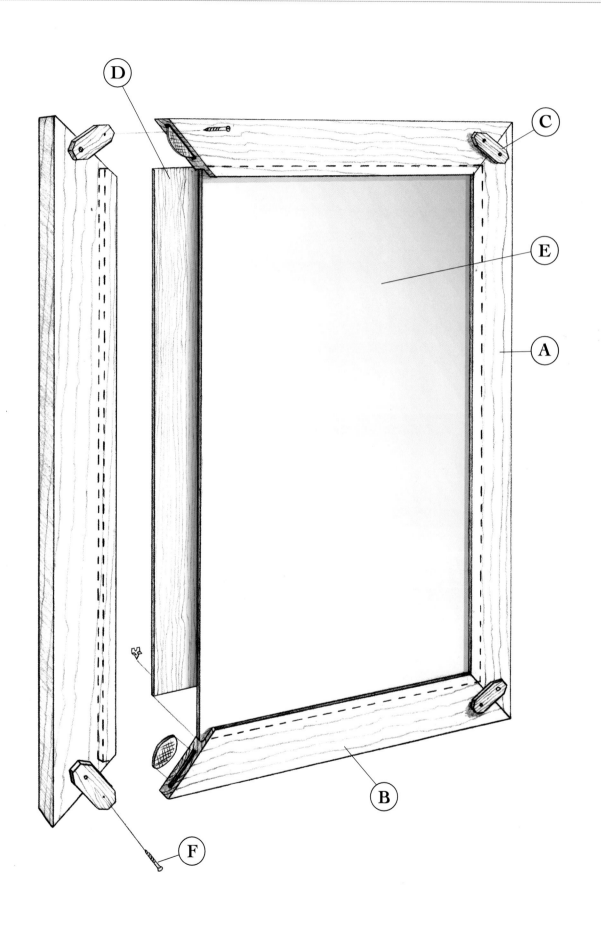

**MATERIALS LIST (INCHES)** • MIRROR FRAME

| REF. | QTY. | PART | MATERIAL | THICKNESS | WIDTH | LENGTH | COMMENTS |
|---|---|---|---|---|---|---|---|
| A | 2 | Long Sides | Sugar Pine | 3/4 | 3 | 36 | |
| B | 2 | Short Sides | Sugar Pine | 3/4 | 3 | 24 | |
| C | 4 | Joint Braces | Sugar Pine | 1/4 | 1 | 3 | |
| D | 1 | Back | Birch Ply | 1/4 | 19 | 31 | |
| E | 1 | Mirror | | 1/4 | 19 | 31 | mirror has cut edges |
| F | 8 | No. 6 x 1/2" Rusted Screws | | | Note: See sidebar for treatment of screws | | |

**MATERIALS LIST (MILLIMETERS)** • MIRROR FRAME

| REF. | QTY. | PART | MATERIAL | THICKNESS | WIDTH | LENGTH | COMMENTS |
|---|---|---|---|---|---|---|---|
| A | 2 | Long Sides | Sugar Pine | 19 | 75 | 915 | |
| B | 2 | Short Sides | Sugar Pine | 19 | 75 | 610 | |
| C | 4 | Joint Braces | Sugar Pine | 6 | 25 | 75 | |
| D | 1 | Back | Birch Ply | 6 | 480 | 785 | |
| E | 1 | Mirror | | 6 | 480 | 785 | mirror has cut edges |
| F | 8 | No. 6 x 12mm Rusted Screws | | | Note: see sidebar for treatment of screws | | |

## ANTIQUING HARDWARE

Unplated hardware works the best when your goal is an antique look. If plated hardware is what you have, simply sand or scrape off the plating. Put the hardware in a plastic or glass container and cover it with vinegar. This will rust the hardware and give it a nice patina. The process can take several days up to a few weeks.

For brass hardware, pour about 1/2" of ammonia into a container. Remove the plating from the hardware and suspend it in a screen hung inside the container. The hardware should not actually touch the ammonia. The fumes will turn the brass all kinds of colors and give it a great-looking patina. This process takes no more than a few hours. Keep the containers outside or in a well-ventilated area.

Steel hardware can be easily aged by dipping it in gun blue (available at most gun stores) for a minute or two. Brass hardware also can be aged using this chemical. First, remove the lacquer from the hardware with lacquer thinner, by sanding, or both. Dip it in gun blue, remove it when black, and then coat the hardware with lacquer.

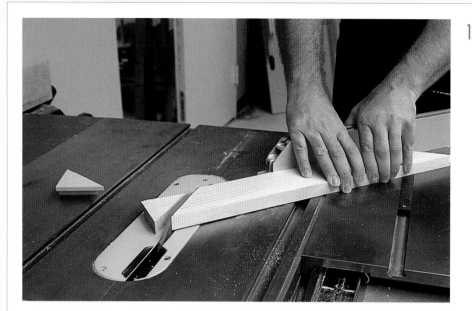

1 | Cutting the 45° angles for the mirror frame is done easily on the table saw. A stop (hidden by my left hand) ensures that like parts are cut to the same lengths.

2 | Cut a ½" × ½" (13mm × 13mm) rabbet on the back inside edge of the frame parts. Make the vertical cut first.

3 | Then make the flat cut.

4 | Biscuits are used at the miter joints to add strength and help align the pieces to each other. Glue up opposite corners of the frame first.

TIP Dipping the biscuits is a quick and easy way to apply the glue. Let some glue drip from the biscuit into the slot before inserting it.

5 | Glue the two assemblies together.

6 | A light brown stain was used because it brings out the rough surface texture. Apply the stain with a brush, let it stand for 1 minute, then wipe off the excess with a rag. Let the stain dry overnight. This project was finished with two coats of satin pre-catalyzed lacquer.

7 | To hold the mirror and backer panel in place, use glazier points.

8 | A sawtooth hanger bracket works great for hanging the frame.

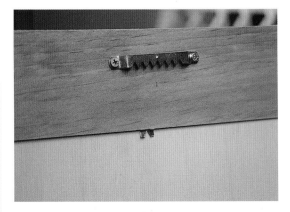

# three-drawer dresser

THIS DRESSER HAS THREE LARGE drawers deep enough to store sweaters, jeans, lots of socks, thermal underwear or a swimsuit. Its metal drawer slides ensure that the drawers will provide years of smooth operating service without sticking or complaining. The top's edges are not cut squarely and the boards for the top, sides and drawer fronts are not edge-glued evenly — all of this adds to the rustic look of the dresser and makes the building process interesting.

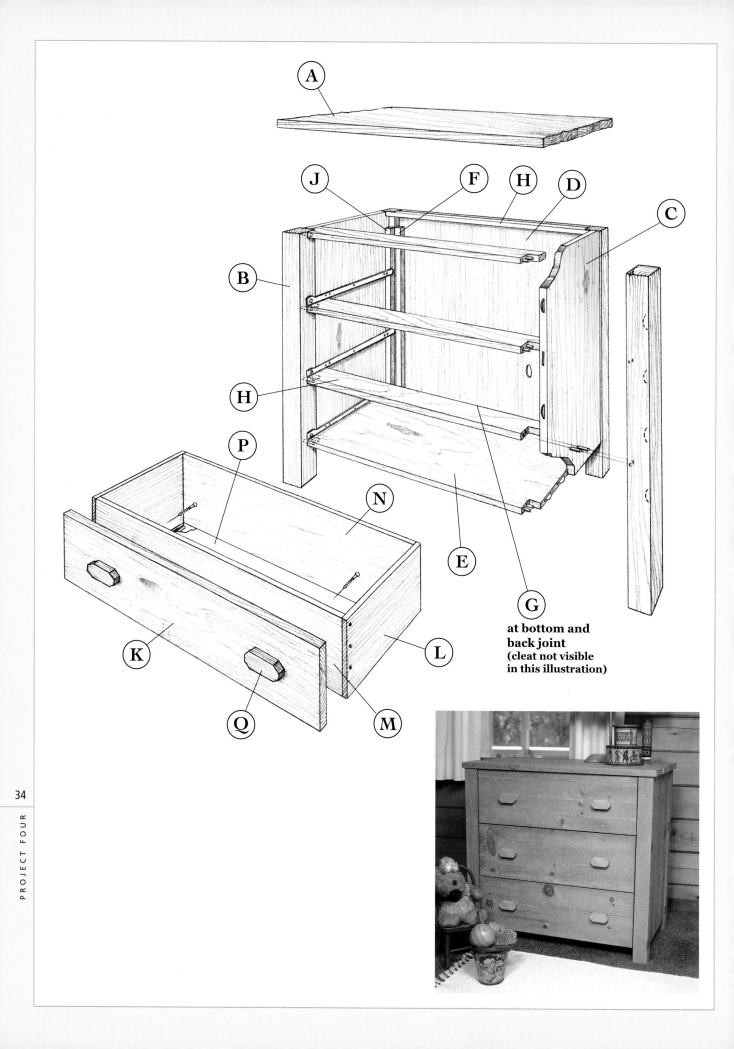

at bottom and
back joint
(cleat not visible
in this illustration)

**MATERIALS LIST (INCHES)** • THREE-DRAWER DRESSER

| REF. | QTY. | PART | MATERIAL | THICKNESS | WIDTH | LENGTH | COMMENTS |
|------|------|------|----------|-----------|-------|--------|----------|
| A | 1 | Top | Sugar Pine | 1 | 20 | 36 | |
| B | 4 | Legs | Sugar Pine | $2\frac{1}{2}$ | $2\frac{1}{2}$ | 32 | |
| C | 2 | Side Panels | Sugar Pine | 1 | $14\frac{1}{2}$ | $29\frac{1}{4}$ (H) | |
| D | 1 | Back Panel | Sugar Pine | 1 | 30 | $29\frac{1}{4}$ (H) | |
| E | 1 | Bottom | Sugar Pine | 1 | 17 | $32\frac{1}{2}$ | |
| F | 2 | Cleats | Soft Maple | 1 | 1 | 24 | |
| G | 1 | Cleat | Soft Maple | 1 | 1 | $29\frac{1}{2}$ | |
| H | 4 | Rails | Sugar Pine | $\frac{7}{8}$ | $3\frac{3}{4}$ | $32\frac{1}{2}$ | |
| J | 2 | Fillers | Sugar Pine | $1\frac{1}{4}$ | $1\frac{1}{4}$ | 24 | |
| K | 3 | Drawer Faces | Sugar Pine | 1 | $9\frac{5}{8}$ | $29\frac{3}{4}$ | |
| L | 6 | Drawer Sides | Soft Maple | $\frac{9}{16}$ | $7\frac{1}{4}$ | 16 | |
| M | 3 | Drawer Fronts | Soft Maple | $\frac{9}{16}$ | $7\frac{1}{4}$ | $27\frac{7}{8}$ | |
| N | 3 | Drawer Backs | Soft Maple | $\frac{9}{16}$ | $6\frac{1}{2}$ | $27\frac{7}{8}$ | |
| P | 3 | Drawer Bottoms | Birch Ply | $\frac{1}{4}$ | $28\frac{1}{4}$ | $15\frac{3}{4}$ | |
| Q | 6 | Drawer Pulls | Sugar Pine | $\frac{3}{4}$ | $1\frac{1}{2}$ | $3\frac{1}{4}$ | |
| | 3 | Sets of 16" Bottom-Mount Drawer Slides | | | | | |
| | 15 | $\frac{1}{2}$" x $\frac{1}{2}$" x 3" Glue Blocks for bottoms of drawers | | | | | |

**MATERIALS LIST (MILLIMETERS)** • THREE-DRAWER DRESSER

| REF. | QTY. | PART | MATERIAL | THICKNESS | WIDTH | LENGTH | COMMENTS |
|------|------|------|----------|-----------|-------|--------|----------|
| A | 1 | Top | Sugar Pine | 25 | 510 | 915 | |
| B | 4 | Legs | Sugar Pine | 65 | 65 | 815 | |
| C | 2 | Side Panels | Sugar Pine | 25 | 370 | 745 (H) | |
| D | 1 | Back Panel | Sugar Pine | 25 | 765 | 745 (H) | |
| E | 1 | Bottom | Sugar Pine | 25 | 430 | 825 | |
| F | 2 | Cleats | Soft Maple | 25 | 25 | 610 | |
| G | 1 | Cleat | Soft Maple | 25 | 25 | 750 | |
| H | 4 | Rails | Sugar Pine | 22 | 95 | 825 | |
| J | 2 | Fillers | Sugar Pine | 32 | 32 | 610 | |
| K | 3 | Drawer Faces | Sugar Pine | 25 | 246 | 760 | |
| L | 6 | Drawer Sides | Soft Maple | 14 | 185 | 400 | |
| M | 3 | Drawer Fronts | Soft Maple | 14 | 185 | 711 | |
| N | 3 | Drawer Backs | Soft Maple | 14 | 165 | 711 | |
| P | 3 | Drawer Bottoms | Birch Ply | 6 | 723 | 392 | |
| Q | 6 | Drawer Pulls | Sugar Pine | 19 | 40 | 85 | |
| | 3 | Sets of 400mm Bottom-Mount Drawer Slides | | | | | |
| | 15 | 13 x 13 x 75 Glue Blocks for bottoms of drawers | | | | | |

1 | The widest board that can be rough-cut resawn is 6" (150mm) with the saw blade that was used. Raise the blade to its full height, cut one half of the board, flip it end for end and cut the other half. (See "How to Create Rough-Sawn Texture" on page 25.) These boards are then glued to make up panels of the needed widths. Don't worry too much about perfection when it comes to leveling the boards to one another. A slight unevenness adds to the rustic look and feel.

2 | Biscuits are used to register and glue the panels to the legs. Note that the legs are glued up to thickness, then planed and rough-cut to size.

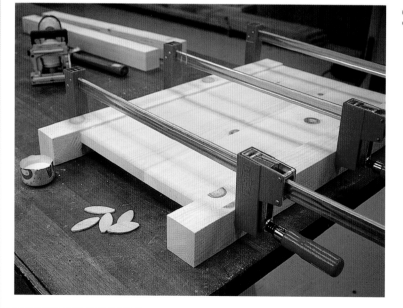

3 | A flat surface makes squaring and gluing the panels easy. Just let the glue set up for 30 minutes and take off the clamps.

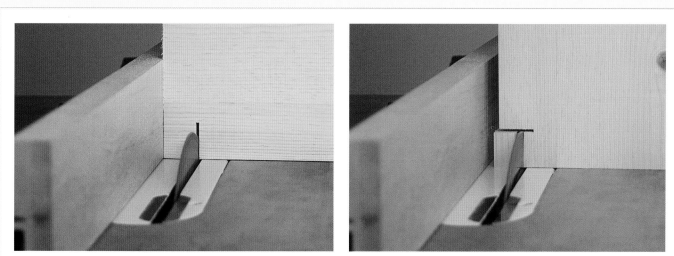

4 | Cut the notches in the bottom and front rails on the table saw as shown in these two photos. Set the fence to the notch width (include the width of the blade in this measurement) and raise the saw blade to the other measurement of the notch. Make the first cut. Flip the piece front to back and onto the other edge of the notch. Adjust the fence and saw blade height if necessary. Make a cut with the panel halfway to the fence, and move the scrap piece out of the way. Then make the full cut and the second scrap piece won't bind in the saw.

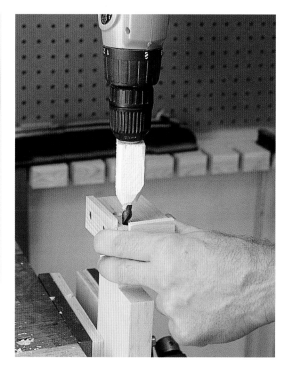

5 | Notch the rails the same way you did for the bottom panel. A homemade doweling jig (see page 14) helps in drilling the holes for the dowels.

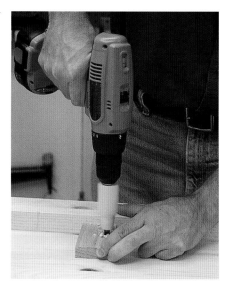

6 | Using the same jig, drill holes for the dowels in the side assemblies.

## MAKING A SQUARE GLUE-UP JIG

First square up one corner of a scrap piece of plywood. Mark that corner so you don't get confused. Set the fence at 4" to 5" from the blade, and make your first cut with the square edge of the panel in the lower right-hand corner. Stop the cut about 4" to 5" from the perpendicular back edge of the panel.

Next flip the panel corner-for-corner and make the second cut.

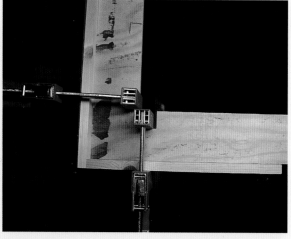

Finally make notches for the clamps and it's ready to go. This is like having an extra set of hands to hold things squarely while the glue sets.

7 | Glue the bottom to one of the sides using biscuits. Check to be sure the side is square to the bottom and adjust the clamps if necessary. If you feel more comfortable, use a square glue-up jig. (See sidebar at left.)

TIP *When attaching any piece of wood cross grain on a solid wood panel, use screws in oversize holes. Never use glue!*

8 | Install cleats on the sides for attaching the back. Drill oversize holes (¼") {6mm} in the cleats for screwing on the back panel. This will allow for movement in the solid wood back panel.

9 | Install spacers for attaching the drawer slides in the back of the cabinet. Be sure to mount the slides squarely to the front face of the cabinet.

10 | Cut all drawer parts as instructed in the materials list. Cut the dadoes for the drawer bottoms in the sides and fronts by setting the table saw fence ½" (13mm) to the blade. Make the first cut in all the sides and fronts.

11 │ Move the fence away from the saw blade approximately ⅛" (3mm) and make the second cut. This cut can be adjusted to make the dado fit the thickness of whatever ¼" (6mm) (plus or minus) material you will be using for the drawer bottoms.

12 │ Attach a square block to your worktop. Stand a drawer side top edge down against one side of the block. Stand a drawer back or front top edge down against the side perpendicular to the drawer side. This block helps register the two drawer parts at right angles to one another. (The drawer sides cover the ends of both the front and back pieces. After the pine drawer fronts are added, the ends of the dadoes will not show.)

**13** Use three 2" (50mm) drywall screws to attach these parts together. You don't need to use glue because screwed joints are very strong. Do this for all drawer parts.

**14** Stand the drawer on its front and slide the drawer bottom into the dado. Put the drawer on its top and square the drawer. Attach the bottom with screws into the bottom of the back.

**15** Add glue blocks for extra strength. Simply put glue on the blocks and push them into place. (No clamps are needed to hold the blocks in place while the glue sets.)

# nightstand

AFTER YOU'VE COMFORTABLY settled into your bed for the evening, you can read that great classic novel by the light of a lamp sitting on this nightstand. (There's also room for some cookies and hot chocolate.) The drawer has room for a pencil and a notebook or a journal.

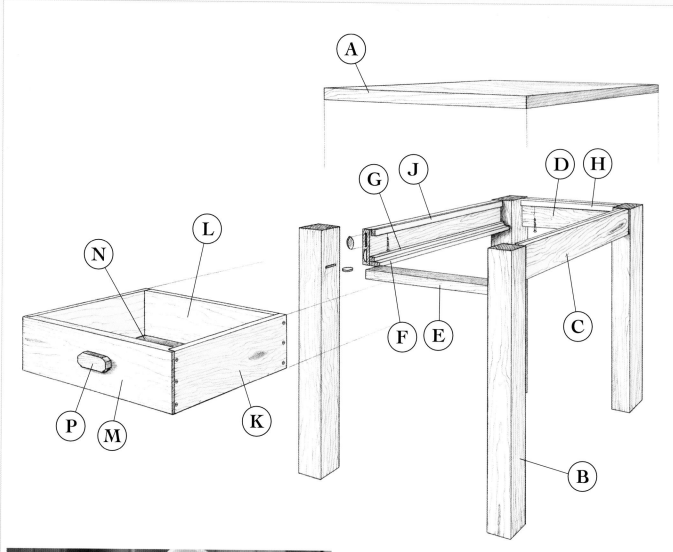

**MATERIALS LIST (INCHES)** • NIGHTSTAND

| REF. | QTY. | PART | MATERIAL | THICKNESS | WIDTH | LENGTH | COMMENTS |
|---|---|---|---|---|---|---|---|
| A | 1 | Top | Sugar Pine | 1 | 18 | 22 | |
| B | 4 | Legs | Sugar Pine | $2\frac{1}{2}$ | $2\frac{1}{2}$ | $27\frac{1}{4}$ | |
| C | 2 | Side Aprons | Sugar Pine | 1 | 5 | 12 | |
| D | 1 | Back Apron | Sugar Pine | 1 | 5 | 15 | |
| E | 1 | Front Rail | Sugar Pine | 1 | $2\frac{1}{2}$ | 15 | |
| F | 2 | Bottom Drawer Glides | Soft Maple | $\frac{3}{4}$ | 2 | $11\frac{1}{2}$ | |
| G | 2 | Side Drawer Glides | Soft Maple | $\frac{3}{4}$ | $\frac{3}{4}$ | $11\frac{1}{2}$ | |
| H | 1 | Back Cleat | Soft Maple | 1 | 1 | $14\frac{1}{2}$ | |
| J | 2 | Side Cleats | Soft Maple | 1 | 1 | $11\frac{1}{2}$ | |
| K | 2 | Drawer Sides | Soft Maple | $\frac{1}{2}$ | 4 | 14 | |
| L | 1 | Drawer Back | Soft Maple | $\frac{1}{2}$ | $3\frac{1}{4}$ | 14 | |
| M | 1 | Drawer Front | Sugar Pine | 1 | 4 | 15 | rough-sawn pine |
| N | 1 | Drawer Bottom | Birch Ply | $\frac{1}{4}$ | $14\frac{1}{2}$ | $13\frac{3}{4}$ | |
| P | 1 | Drawer Pull | Sugar Pine | $\frac{3}{4}$ | $1\frac{1}{2}$ | $3\frac{1}{4}$ | |
| | 3 | $\frac{1}{2}$" x $\frac{1}{2}$" x 3" Glue Blocks for bottom of drawer | | | | | |

**MATERIALS LIST (MILLIMETERS)** • NIGHTSTAND

| REF. | QTY. | PART | MATERIAL | THICKNESS | WIDTH | LENGTH | COMMENTS |
|---|---|---|---|---|---|---|---|
| A | 1 | Top | Sugar Pine | 25 | 455 | 560 | |
| B | 4 | Legs | Sugar Pine | 65 | 65 | 690 | |
| C | 2 | Side Aprons | Sugar Pine | 25 | 130 | 305 | |
| D | 1 | Back Apron | Sugar Pine | 25 | 130 | 380 | |
| E | 1 | Front Rail | Sugar Pine | 25 | 65 | 380 | |
| F | 2 | Bottom Drawer Glides | Soft Maple | 19 | 50 | 290 | |
| G | 2 | Side Drawer Glides | Soft Maple | 19 | 19 | 290 | |
| H | 1 | Back Cleat | Soft Maple | 25 | 25 | 370 | |
| J | 2 | Side Cleats | Soft Maple | 25 | 25 | 290 | |
| K | 2 | Drawer Sides | Soft Maple | 12.5 | 100 | 355 | |
| L | 1 | Drawer Back | Soft Maple | 12.5 | 80 | 355 | |
| M | 1 | Drawer Front | Sugar Pine | 25 | 100 | 380 | rough-sawn pine |
| N | 1 | Drawer Bottom | Birch Ply | 6 | 365 | 350 | |
| P | 1 | Drawer Pull | Sugar Pine | 19 | 40 | 85 | |
| | 3 | 13 x 13 x 75 Glue Blocks for bottom of drawer | | | | | |

1 | Biscuits work very well for aligning and holding this project together. Make the slots for the aprons and the lower front rail. Be sure all the legs have slots on two adjacent sides.

2 | Glue up the two side assemblies first.

3 | Glue the two side assemblies together. Glue on the cleats for attaching the top.

4 | Preassemble the runner assemblies and glue them into place. Be sure the side runners are slightly proud of the inside of the front legs. This will allow the drawer to slide in and out without rubbing the legs. The lower runner should be level with the front rail. Make sure the runners are parallel with each other.

5 | Attach the top with screws through the mounting cleats. Do not use glue. Then fit the drawer to the opening. It is easier to fit each drawer side individually, making the necessary adjustments as needed before assembling the drawer.

6 | The drawer sides and back are made the same way the drawer parts for the dresser are made (see the chapter "Three-Drawer Dresser," which begins on page 32.) The front has rabbets on each end that accept the sides. Set the table saw fence at ½" {13mm} (including the blade thickness) and the blade height at ½" {13mm} (the thickness of the drawer sides). Stand the drawer front on end with the inside face against the fence and make the first cut for the rabbet in each end.

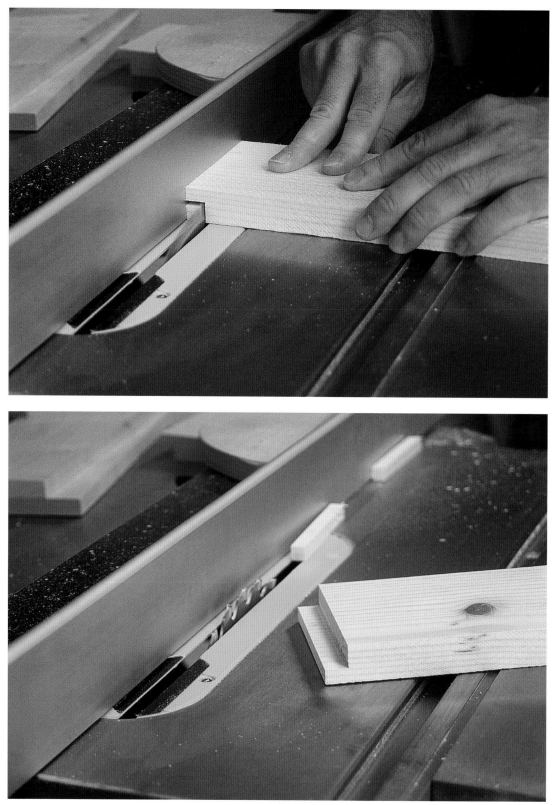

7 | Lay the drawer front face up and make the second rabbet cut as shown
here. (Always use a scrap of wood to test your cuts.)

8 | Assemble the drawer with screws. Make any fitting adjustments needed using a belt sander and/or a block plane.

9 | Detail of fitted drawer.

# dry sink cabinet

THIS CABINET IS BASED ON A DRY SINK cabinet. But since the top does not open, the upper inside of the cabinet is available for storage. If you happen to have a television in your cabin (perish the thought!), this project could make an excellent small entertainment center. Or, by adding a shelf or two, it could be used in the kitchen for extra storage or in the bedroom as a dresser with doors.

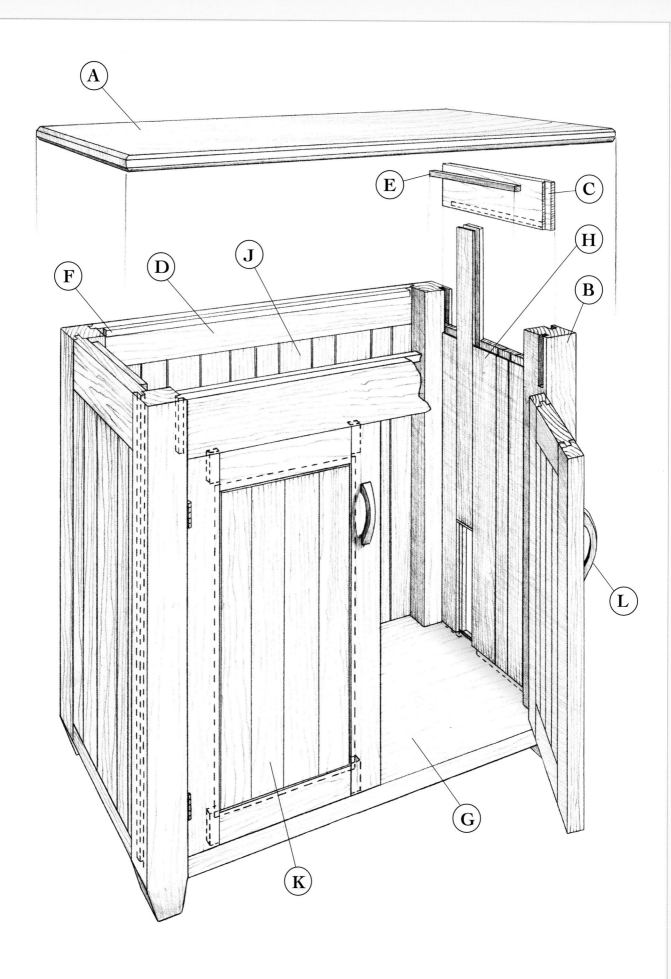

## MATERIALS LIST (INCHES) • DRY SINK CABINET

| REF. | QTY. | PART | MATERIAL | THICKNESS | WIDTH | LENGTH | COMMENTS |
|---|---|---|---|---|---|---|---|
| A | 1 | Top | Sugar Pine | $1^{1}/_4$ | $21^{1}/_4$ | $41^{1}/_4$ | |
| B | 4 | Legs | Sugar Pine | $2^{5}/_8$ | $2^{5}/_8$ | 37 | |
| C | 2 | Side Top Rails | Sugar Pine | 1 | $3^{7}/_8$ | 15 | $^{1}/_2$" tenons on each end |
| D | 2 | Front & Back Rails | Sugar Pine | 1 | $3^{7}/_8$ | 33 | $^{1}/_2$" tenons on each end |
| E | 2 | Cleats | Sugar Pine | $^{3}/_4$ | $^{3}/_4$ | 12 | |
| F | 2 | Cleats | Sugar Pine | $^{3}/_4$ | $^{3}/_4$ | $27^{1}/_2$ | |
| G | 1 | Bottom | Sugar Pine | 1 | $19^{1}/_4$ | $37^{1}/_4$ | |
| H | 2 | Side Panels | Sugar Pine | $^{3}/_4$ | $14^{1}/_2$ | $29^{1}/_2$ (H) | |
| J | 1 | Back Panel | Sugar Pine | $^{3}/_4$ | $32^{1}/_2$ | $29^{1}/_2$ (H) | |
| K { | 2 | Doors | Sugar Pine | $^{7}/_8$ | $15^{13}/_{16}$ | $28^{13}/_{16}$ | Finished dimensions of doors. |
| | 4 | Stiles | Sugar Pine | $^{7}/_8$ | $2^{1}/_8$ | $28^{13}/_{16}$ | |
| | 4 | Rails | Sugar Pine | $^{7}/_8$ | $2^{1}/_8$ | $12^{9}/_{16}$ | |
| | 2 | Panels | Sugar Pine | $^{5}/_8$ | $12^{7}/_{16}$ | $24^{7}/_{16}$ | |
| L | 2 | Door Handles | Sugar Pine | $^{3}/_4$ | $1^{1}/_8$ | 4 | |
| | 2 pair | $1^{1}/_2$" x 2" Rusted Hinges and Screws (see sidebar "Antiquing Hardware" on page 29) | | | | | |

## MATERIALS LIST (MILLIMETERS) • DRY SINK CABINET

| REF. | QTY. | PART | MATERIAL | THICKNESS | WIDTH | LENGTH | COMMENTS |
|---|---|---|---|---|---|---|---|
| A | 1 | Top | Sugar Pine | 32 | 540 | 1050 | |
| B | 4 | Legs | Sugar Pine | 65 | 65 | 940 | |
| C | 2 | Side Top Rails | Sugar Pine | 25 | 100 | 380 | 12.5mm tenons on each end |
| D | 2 | Front & Back Rails | Sugar Pine | 25 | 100 | 840 | 12.5mm tenons on each end |
| E | 2 | Cleats | Sugar Pine | 19 | 19 | 300 | |
| F | 2 | Cleats | Sugar Pine | 19 | 19 | 700 | |
| G | 1 | Bottom | Sugar Pine | 25 | 485 | 945 | |
| H | 2 | Side Panels | Sugar Pine | 19 | 367 | 750 (H) | |
| J | 1 | Back Panel | Sugar Pine | 19 | 945 | 750 (H) | |
| K { | 2 | Doors | Sugar Pine | 22 | 404 | 733 | Finished dimensions of doors. |
| | 4 | Stiles | Sugar Pine | 22 | 55 | 733 | |
| | 4 | Rails | Sugar Pine | 22 | 55 | 319 | |
| | 2 | Panels | Sugar Pine | 16 | 306 | 635 | |
| L | 2 | Door Handles | Sugar Pine | 19 | 30 | 100 | |
| | 2 pair | 40mm x 50mm Rusted Hinges and Screws (see sidebar "Antiquing Hardware" on page 29) | | | | | |

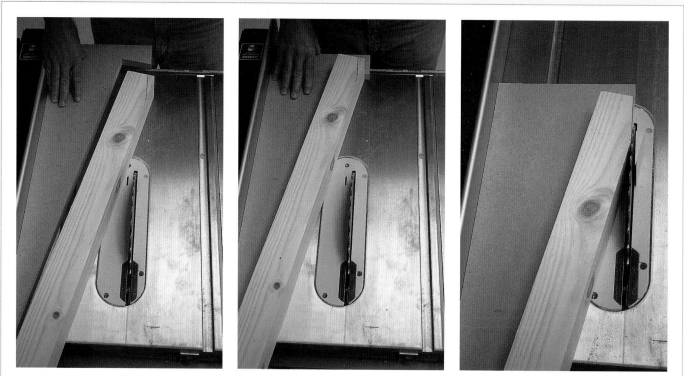

1 | Using a tapering jig, cut the bevels on the legs as shown here.

2 | To make all four cuts, simply turn the leg to the next face.

3 | Set the fence and the saw blade height using a scrap piece of wood to make your test cuts. Then, make the first cut in the panel.

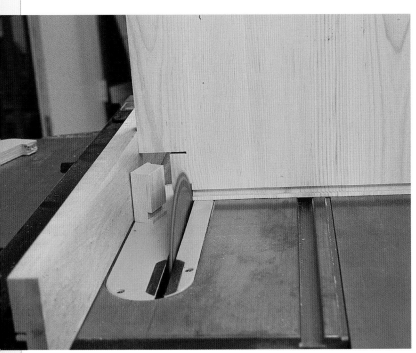

**4** Turn the panel front to back, adjust the fence and saw blade height if necessary. Then make the final cutout in two passes. (This will prevent the falloff from binding between the fence and the saw blade.) Note: The dadoes have already been cut in the bottom panel and in the legs. However, it was determined that a better course would be to cut them later in the sequence when the ¼" (6mm) dado is set up, so all dadoing can be done at the same time.

**5** Use a doweling jig (see sidebar "Making a Homemade Doweling Jig" on page 14) to drill the holes for the dowels in the notch in the bottom panel. (Above, my thumb is registering the edge of the jig flush with the bottom edge of the panel.)

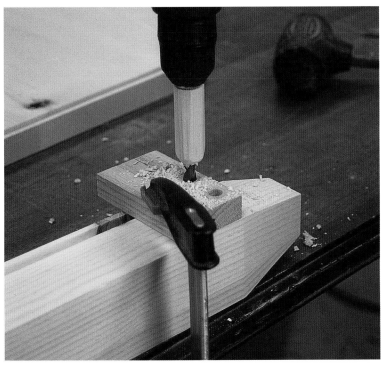

**6** Register the end of the jig where the inside of the cutout will meet the leg. Also register the side of the jig where the bottom will meet the foot (this is at the start of the bevel on the foot of the leg).

**7** This shows the setup of the dado cutter without the center chippers. Put a ¼" (6mm) spacer in between the two dado blades. This setup will create the tongue for the tongue-and-groove joinery.

8 | Using the stock throat plate that came with your table saw as a template, make a new throat plate out of ½" (13mm) Baltic birch. Attach a sacrificial fence to the table saw fence. Set the fence so the inside of the dado blade barely cuts into the fence.

9 | Using scrap wood the same thickness as the panel pieces, make test cuts until the setup cuts the tongue in the center of the panel pieces. Remember to cut the tongue on only one long edge of each panel piece.

10 | Stand the panel pieces on end and cut tongues on both ends of each piece. (Note the backer piece of wood behind the panel piece. This helps to stabilize the panel while making the cut. Also note the importance of making the throat plate. It stops the narrow panel piece from falling into the dado cutter.)

11 | Change the dado setup by removing the spacer between the blades. Set up the dado to cut a ¼" (6mm) groove. Use the scrap wood test piece to set up the groove in the center of the panel piece. Cut all grooves in the cabinet's bottom panel and top rails (as shown in the drawings) at this time while the dado is set up. Also cut the dadoes in the legs at this time. Cut the tenons on the ends of the top rails (see "Making the Panel Doors" in this chapter for information about cutting the tenons).

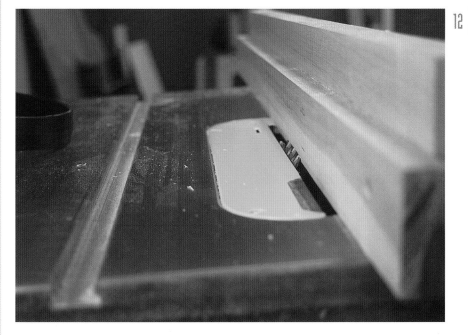

12 | Reverse the fence setup and put it on the opposite side of the saw blade. Tilt the saw blade to 45°.

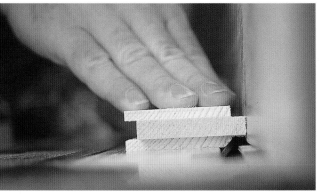

13 | Using your test scrap of wood, adjust the setup for cutting the shoulder bevels on the tongue edge of the panel pieces until it cuts as shown in the photo.

14 | Using a test scrap of wood, adjust the setup for cutting the shoulder bevels on the dado edge of the panel pieces until it cuts as shown above.

15 | The finished panel should look like this. Random-size panel pieces give a less rigid look and feel to the side and back panels.

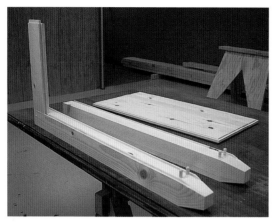

16 | When the tongue-and-groove panels have been made to size and all parts have been dry fitted, proceed with gluing up a cabinet side assembly. The bottom panel is part of the side panel assembly. (Note that the tongue-and-groove panels are not glued to the bottom panel or top rail. These pieces will float in the final assembly.)

17 | The cabinet side assembly can be easily put together and clamped up by one person.

19 | The top is attached with screws and no glue.

18 | When the glue has set up, the back panel, the back top rail and the other end panel can be attached to complete the assembly of the cabinet body. Remember to let the back and side panels float.

# MAKING A PANEL DOOR

1 | To cut grooves in the frame parts, set the table saw fence ¼" (6mm) from the inside edge of the saw blade. Set the blade height to ½" (13mm). Cut a groove in one long edge of all frame parts. Reset the fence to ⅜" (9mm) and make the second cut for the groove. This will create a ¼"-wide (6mm-wide) groove.

2 | Set the table saw fence at ¹⁵⁄₃₂" (12mm) from the fence to the outside of the saw blade. (This will cut the tenon length to a length slightly less than the depth of the dado.) Set the saw blade to a height of ¼" (6mm). Using the miter gauge to feed the work, nibble the material away to create half of the tenon. Make this cut on both ends of all the rails.

4 | This is how the tenon will look. Keep track of which face is the outside of all the door parts. The dado and tenon are not centered on the parts. This is so the ⅝" (16mm) door panel can be properly set to have its face flush with the door frame.

3 | Flip the rails face down and make the second nibbling cut. Reset the saw blade height if necessary to make the tenon the correct thickness.

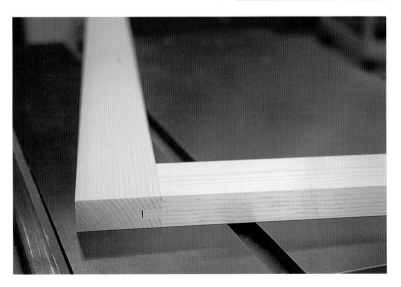

5 | The assembled mortise-and-tenon joint is shown here. The space at the end of the tenon is for excess glue that will get forced into the joint. (Cut extra frame material to use as test pieces for setting up and making the cuts. Getting the cuts right on a piece of scrap saves you a lot of headaches later on.)

6 | To create the lip on the door panel, set the table saw fence ¼" (6mm) from the inside of the saw blade to the fence. Raise the saw blade to ½" (13mm). Stand the panel on edge with the inside of the panel against the fence. Make cuts on all four edges of the panel.

7 | Reset the the fence to ½" (13mm) from the outside of the saw blade to the fence. Check the height of the saw blade to make sure it doesn't cut into the tenon of the panel. Lay the panel on its face and make four cuts around the edges of the panel.

9 | Sand the panel prior to assembly. Gather all the door parts together and lay them out in order. Stand a stile on edge, apply glue to a rail tenon and put it in place on the stile.

8 | This is how the panel will look when you're finished.

10 | Insert the panel into the grooves, glue up the other rail's tenon and put it in place. (Do not put glue on the panel.) Apply glue on the two remaining tenons and put the other stile in place.

11 | Check the assembly for squareness and make sure the reveal around all edges of the panel is even. Adjust the panel with a wood block and a hammer if needed. Clamp the assembly, applying light pressure. Double-check for squareness again and apply firm clamping pressure.

12 | Put the hinges on the doors. Open the hinge and fold it back until the barrel is tight against the front edge of the door. A good rule of thumb: Place the ends of the hinges 3" down from the top edge of the door and 3" up from the bottom edge of the door.

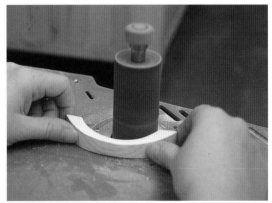

14 | If you would like to use the handles shown on this project, here's how to make them. Trace the pattern onto the wood. Cut out the curves on the band saw, leaving the tracing lines visible.

13 | Measure from the front face of the door to the centerline of the hinge screws and transfer that measurement to the side of the cabinet. Draw a centerline on the side of the cabinet and use it as a reference for screwing the door to the cabinet.

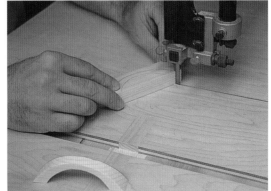

15 | Use a spindle sander to smooth the curves. Then stand the handle up and cut the narrowing curves on the band saw. Smooth these cuts on the spindle sander. Attach the handles to the door with screws from the inside of the door.

# branch chair

THIS CHAIR IS A LOT OF FUN TO MAKE.
Gathering the materials is a big part of the experience. As I was gathering branches
and old roots, I felt like I was getting
back to the source of what woodworking is all about. As I walked among the
trees, I felt like I was being given these
materials as gifts from the trees them-
selves. As you build this project, take the
time to enjoy the whole experience!

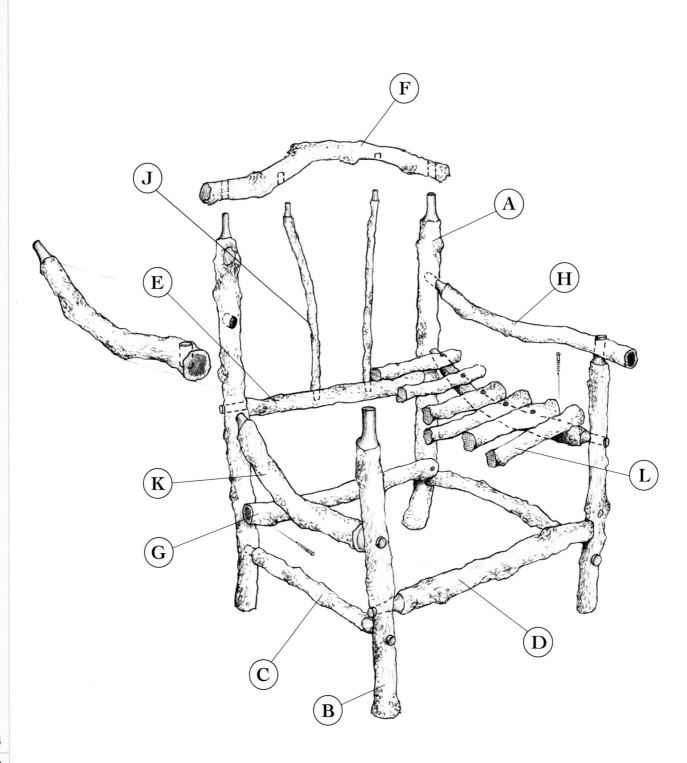

**MATERIALS LIST (INCHES)** • BRANCH CHAIR

| REF. | QTY. | PART | MATERIAL | DIAMETER | LENGTH | COMMENTS |
|---|---|---|---|---|---|---|
| A | 2 | Back Legs | Ash Branches | 2 | 34$^+$/- | |
| B | 2 | Front Legs | Ash Branches | 2 | 24$^+$/- | |
| C | 2 | Side Rungs | Ash Branches | 1$^1$/$_2$ | 22$^+$/- | |
| D | 1 | Front Rungs | Ash Branches | 1$^1$/$_2$ | 26$^+$/- | |
| E | 1 | Back Rail | Ash Branches | 1$^1$/$_2$ | 24$^+$/- | |
| F | 1 | Crest Rail | Ash Branches | 1$^1$/$_2$ | 26$^+$/- | |
| G | 1 | Back Rung | Ash Branches | 1$^1$/$_2$ | 24$^+$/- | |
| H | 2 | Arms | Ash Branches | 2 | 26$^+$/- | |
| J | 2 | Vertical Back Rails | Ash Branches | $^3$/$_4$ | 18$^+$/- | |
| K | 2 | Seat Side Rails | Ash Branches | 1$^1$/$_2$ | 22$^+$/- | |
| L | 6-7 | Seat Rails | Ash Branches | 1$^1$/$_2$ | 24-26$^+$/- | back to front lengths |

**MATERIALS LIST (MILLIMETERS)** • BRANCH CHAIR

| REF. | QTY. | PART | MATERIAL | DIAMETER | LENGTH | COMMENTS |
|---|---|---|---|---|---|---|
| A | 2 | Back Legs | Ash Branches | 50 | 865$^+$/- | |
| B | 2 | Front Legs | Ash Branches | 50 | 610$^+$/- | |
| C | 2 | Side Rungs | Ash Branches | 38 | 560$^+$/- | |
| D | 1 | Front Rung | Ash Branches | 38 | 660$^+$/- | |
| E | 1 | Back Rail | Ash Branches | 38 | 610$^+$/- | |
| F | 1 | Crest Rail | Ash Branches | 38 | 660$^+$/- | |
| G | 1 | Back Rung | Ash Branches | 38 | 610$^+$/- | |
| H | 2 | Arms | Ash Branches | 50 | 660/- | |
| J | 2 | Vertical Back Rails | Ash Branches | 19 | 460$^+$/- | |
| K | 2 | Seat Side Rails | Ash Branches | 38 | 560$^+$/- | |
| L | 6-7 | Seat Rails | Ash Branches | 38 | 610-660$^+$/- | back to front lengths |

This is where you begin. Spread out your materials and start imagining the possibilities! This is fun and gets the creative juices flowing.

3 | Cutting the tenons using the tenon cutter. This is a great tool that makes this work even more fun and easy.

2 | After beginning with a basic design and finding the pieces you'd like to use, start trimming off the excess twigs and growths that don't appeal to you. This is very subjective work. Go with your instincts.

4 | There may be times when the angles are steep and a little extra trimming on the shoulders of the tenons is needed.

5 | Drilling the holes for the tenons is the trickiest part of the construction process. Mark each one as you progress. You will find the designing never stops as you keep moving along with the construction.

6 | Drilling the holes is an eye/hand coordinated effort. A few test drillings before you launch into the project will help you get the feel for how this works.

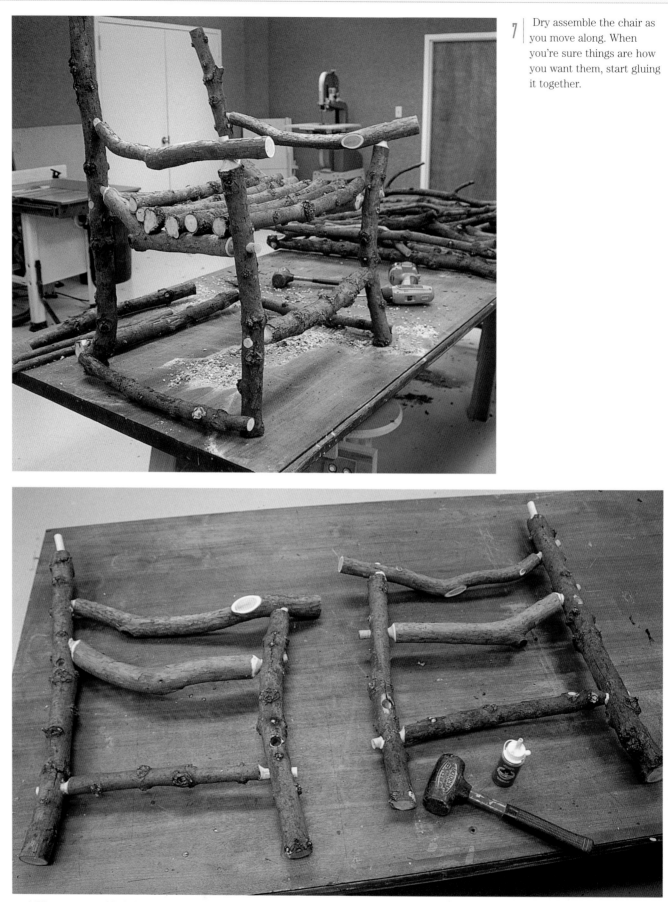

8 | The two assembled chair sides are shown here. Use polyurethane glue to assemble them. This glue is attracted to moisture, so with the moisture still in the branches, it creates very solid joints.

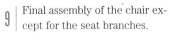

9 | Final assembly of the chair except for the seat branches.

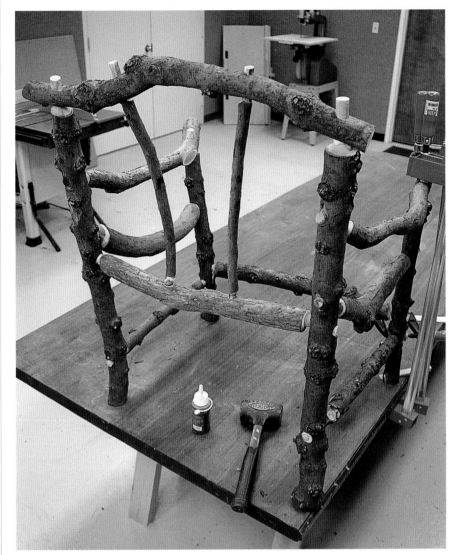

10 | Cut seat slats to length and smooth the ends. Screw the seat slats into place using outdoor deck screws. Three coats of satin pre-catalyzed lacquer were used to finish this project. However, if it will be outside, use polyurethane, spar varnish or any wood deck sealer as a finish.

# branch mirror frame

THIS FRAME SHOWS HOW EASY IT IS TO BE creative with branch construction. Think of this mirror frame as a "jumping-off" point for your own design. The techniques used in making this mirror are the same as those used in constructing the branch chair. One solution for attaching the mirror to the frame is shown but, depending on your design, you may need to create another method for this attachment.

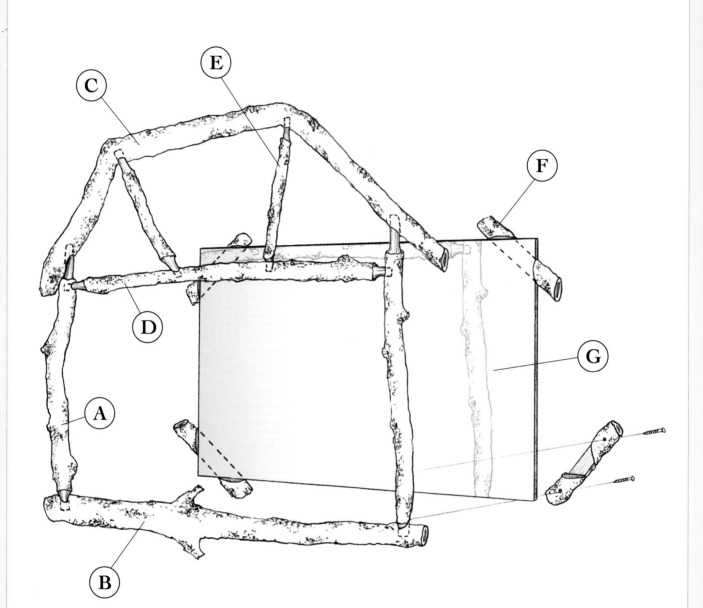

**MATERIALS LIST (INCHES) • BRANCH MIRROR FRAME**

| REF. | QTY. | PART | MATERIAL | DIAMETER | LENGTH | COMMENTS |
|---|---|---|---|---|---|---|
| A | 2 | Sides | Ash Branches | 1$^{1}/_{2}$ | 28$^{+}$/- | |
| B | 1 | Bottom | Ash Branches | 1$^{1}/_{2}$ | 34$^{+}$/- | |
| C | 1 | Top Crest Rail | Ash Branches | 1$^{1}/_{2}$ | 34$^{+}$/- | |
| D | 1 | Top | Ash Branches | 1$^{1}/_{2}$ | 32$^{+}$/- | |
| E | 2 | Vertical Stiles | Ash Branches | 1 | 8-12$^{+}$/- | |
| F | 4 | Corner Braces | Ash Branches | 1 | 6-8$^{+}$/- | right angle cut out for mirror corner |
| G | 1 | Mirror $^{1}/_{4}$" x 20" x 30" with cut edges | | | | |

**MATERIALS LIST (MILLIMETERS) • BRANCH MIRROR FRAME**

| REF. | QTY. | PART | MATERIAL | DIAMETER | LENGTH | COMMENTS |
|---|---|---|---|---|---|---|
| A | 2 | Sides | Ash Branches | 38 | 715$^{+}$/- | |
| B | 1 | Bottom | Ash Branches | 38 | 860$^{+}$/- | |
| C | 1 | Top Crest Rail | Ash Branches | 38 | 860$^{+}$/- | |
| D | 1 | Top | Ash Branches | 38 | 810$^{+}$/- | |
| E | 2 | Vertical Stiles | Ash Branches | 25 | 200-300$^{+}$/- | |
| F | 4 | Corner Braces | Ash Branches | 25 | 150-200$^{+}$/- | right angle cut out for mirror corner |
| G | 1 | Mirror 6 x 500 x 760 with cut edges | | | | |

1 | When the frame is assembled, holding the mirror in place may be a challenge because the frame may not be perfectly flat. The mirror "floats" on the frame.

2 | Cut four brackets to shape on the band saw, or use a coping saw.

**3** Do not over-tighten the screws in the brackets. This could create excess pressure that would cause the mirror to twist and break as you screwed the brackets into place. If you feel uncomfortable using a screw gun, use a standard screwdriver powered by your own hand.

**4** The finished mirror frame with the brackets in place turned out to be a very sturdy project.

# game table

THIS IS ABOUT AS SIMPLE AS IT GETS
for building a table — four legs and a top.
The fun part of this project is finding just
the right legs. The possibilities are almost end-
less: Straight, curved, crooked or twisted legs
would all work for this table. It's designed to
be used as a small game table, but would func-
tion very well as a coffee table or an end table.
The through-tenons are strong and provide a
visual treat.

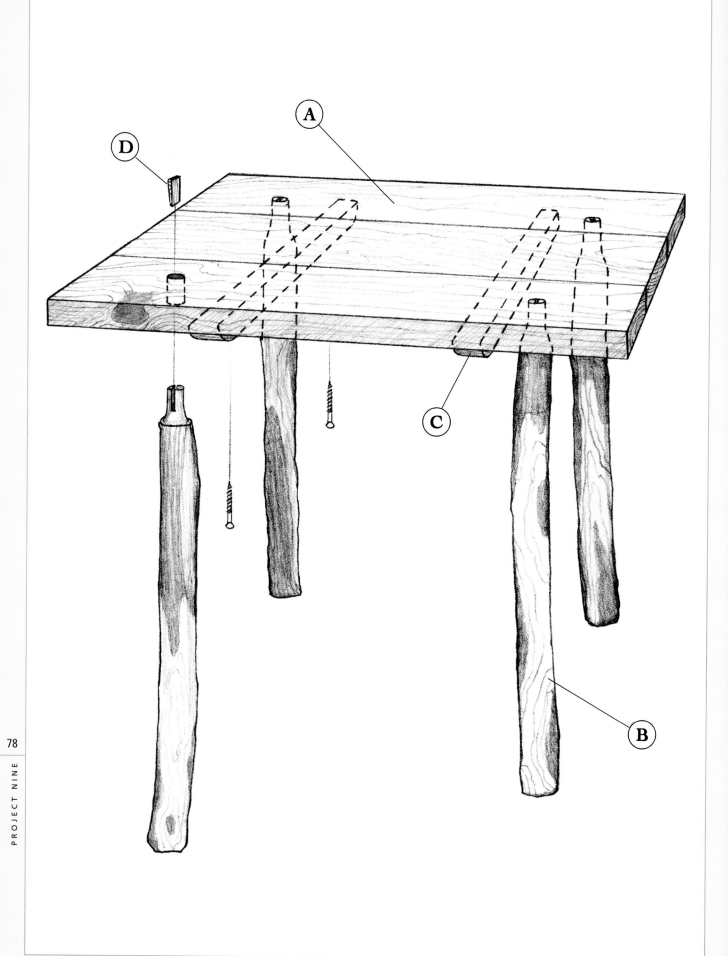

**MATERIALS LIST (INCHES)** • GAME TABLE

| REF. | QTY. | PART | MATERIAL | THICK | WIDTH | LENGTH | COMMENTS |
|------|------|------|----------|-------|-------|--------|----------|
| A | 1 | Top | Yellow Pine | $1^{1}/_{4}$ | 26 | 26 | |
| B | 4 | Legs | Ash Poles | 2 dia. | | 23 | $^{3}/_{4}$" x $1^{1}/_{2}$" tenon one end |
| C | 2 | Battens | Yellow Pine | 1 | 2 | $21^{1}/_{2}$ | |
| D | 4 | Wedges | Yellow Pine | $^{1}/_{8}$ - $^{1}/_{4}$ | $^{3}/_{4}$ | $1^{1}/_{2}$ | |
| | 6 | No. 8 x 3" Screws | | | | | |
| | 6 | $^{3}/_{8}$" Flat Washers | | | | | |

**MATERIALS LIST (MILLIMETERS)** • GAME TABLE

| REF. | QTY. | PART | MATERIAL | THICK | WIDTH | LENGTH | COMMENTS |
|------|------|------|----------|-------|-------|--------|----------|
| A | 1 | Top | Yellow Pine | 32 | 660 | 660 | |
| B | 4 | Legs | Ash Poles | 50 dia. | | 585 | 19mm x 38mm tenon on one end |
| C | 2 | Battens | Yellow Pine | 25 | 50 | 545 | |
| D | 4 | Wedges | Yellow Pine | 3-6 | 19 | 38 | |
| | 6 | No. 8 x 75mm Screws | | | | | |
| | 6 | 9.5mm Flat Washers | | | | | |

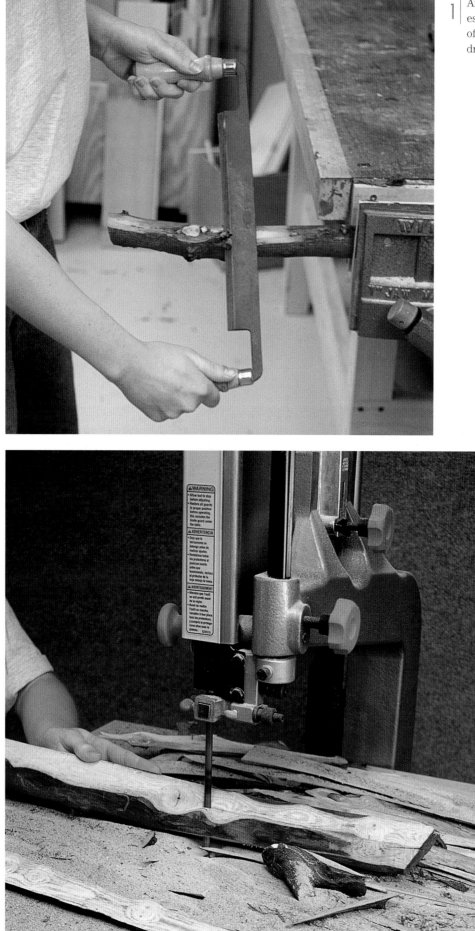

1 | After choosing four branches to use for the legs, peel off the bark using a drawknife.

2 | The band saw can also be used to strip the bark off of a branch. It is like peeling a carrot. Leave the saw marks. They add to the rough look.

3 | After cutting the tenons on the tops of all the legs, cut notches for the wedges using the band saw or a handsaw.

4 | A detail of the finished notch. Cut wedges to fit in the notches.

5 | The top is made of yellow pine. After gluing it up and cutting to size, locate and drill ¾" holes for the leg tenons. If you want the legs to splay a bit, drill the holes at slight angles. Apply glue to the tenon and insert in the hole. Put glue on the wedges and drive them home. When the glue is dry, trim the tenons flush with the top, sand and finish. This project was finished with three coats of clear satin pre-catalyzed lacquer.

# basic bookcase

THIS PROJECT OFFERS AN UNCOMPLICATED
approach to making a very sturdy bookcase. Put
all those novels you have loved reading, and all
those you want to read, on the shelves of this
bookcase, where they will be always within
reach. You can curl up by the fire with one of
them and let your imagination carry you away.

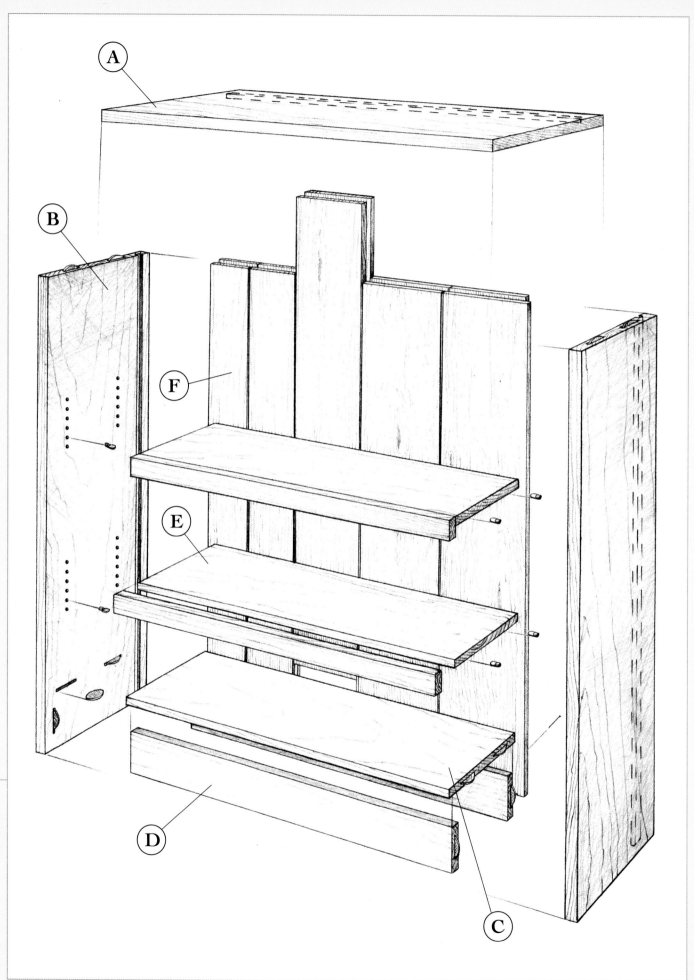

**MATERIALS LIST (INCHES)** • BASIC BOOKCASE

| REF. | QTY. | PART | MATERIAL | THICKNESS | WIDTH | LENGTH | COMMENTS |
|---|---|---|---|---|---|---|---|
| A | 1 | Top | Sugar Pine | $3/4$ | 11 | 32 | |
| B | 2 | Sides | Sugar Pine | $3/4$ | $10^{1}/_{2}$ | $35^{1}/_{4}$ | |
| C | 1 | Bottom | Sugar Pine | $3/4$ | $9^{7}/_{8}$ | $28^{1}/_{2}$ | |
| D | 2 | Bases | Sugar Pine | $3/4$ | 3 | $28^{1}/_{2}$ | |
| E | 2 | Shelves | Sugar Pine | $3/4$ | $9^{3}/_{4}$ | $28^{7}/_{16}$ | glue $1/2$" x $1^{1}/_{2}$" x $28^{7}/_{16}$" strip on front edge |
| F | 1 | Back | Sugar Pine | $1/2$ | 29 | $32^{1}/_{2}$ | made of random-width panels |
| | 8 | Shelf Pins with Insert Collars | | | | | |

**MATERIALS LIST (MILLIMETERS)** • BASIC BOOKCASE

| REF. | QTY. | PART | MATERIAL | THICKNESS | WIDTH | LENGTH | COMMENTS |
|---|---|---|---|---|---|---|---|
| A | 1 | Top | Sugar Pine | 19 | 280 | 810 | |
| B | 2 | Sides | Sugar Pine | 19 | 270 | 895 | |
| C | 1 | Bottom | Sugar Pine | 19 | 257 | 725 | |
| D | 2 | Bases | Sugar Pine | 19 | 75 | 725 | |
| E | 2 | Shelves | Sugar Pine | 19 | 265 | 723 | glue 13 x 40 x 723 strip on front edge |
| F | 1 | Back | Sugar Pine | 13 | 737 | 820 | made of random-width panels |
| | 8 | Shelf Pins with Insert Collars | | | | | |

1 After cutting all parts as shown in the Materials List, draw the layout lines for the dadoes in the two side panels and lay them with the back edges together. This simple step is an easy way to be sure you end up with a right and left side. Draw a line showing where the top edge of the bottom panel will be located. Also draw lines where the dadoes will be located.

2 Lay a side panel on your assembly table with the layout lines showing. Put the corresponding end of the bottom panel in line with the layout line on the side (i.e., the left side panel and the left end of the bottom will go together). The bottom panel should be topside down on the side panel with its edge lined up with the layout line. Clamp this assembly in place. Mark where the biscuits will be located. Line up the biscuit joiner flat on the side and cut the slots in the bottom panel edge.

3 Stand the joiner up, rest the base against the edge of the bottom panel, and cut the slots in the side panel. This setup makes it easy to cut the slots in the two mated pieces very quickly and accurately. Do this same setup for the other side. Create a similar layout for joining the top to the sides.

4 | Set up a router with a ¼" (6mm) straight bit and a fence. Rout a ¼"-deep (6mm-deep) dado in each side as marked. Make a stopped dado cut in the top panel using the same setup.

5 | Glue the two baseboards to the bottom panel.

6 | Attach the sides to the bottom assembly first. Notice the top has been put into place to help keep the unit square.

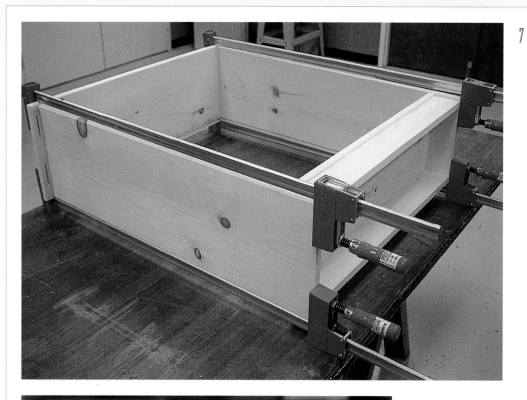

**7** To glue the top into place, put two clamps on the assembly table, glue up the top and attach it to the sides. Lay this assembly on the clamps. Put two more clamps on the top of the assembly, tighten all the clamps and let the glue dry. Double-check for squareness.

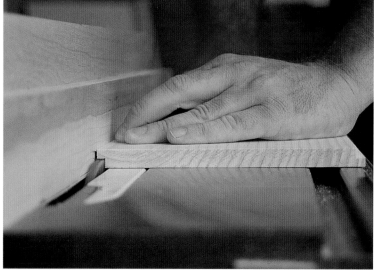

**8** The panels for the back of the bookcase can be made in random widths. To cut the rabbets for the shiplap joints, set up the dado blade cutter in the table saw using the sacrificial fence as shown in the photo. Cut a rabbet on the edge of a panel. Turn over the panel and cut a rabbet on the other edge. Note that the rabbets are on opposite faces of the panel.

**9** The back panels are inserted from the bottom of the bookcase and are held in place by a single screw (in the center of each panel) that is inserted into the back edge of the bottom panel. Do not use any glue.

10 | Make a drilling template, and drill holes for the shelf pins.

11 | Attach the stiffener strips with glue to the front edges of the shelves. This adds strength to the shelves and gives them a heavier, more solid look.

12 | Detail of a shelf pin and its collar insert. This type of shelf pin is very good for working with softwoods. It provides ample strength without tearing out the hole.

# dining table & stools

A ROUND TABLE SEATS MORE people than a square table with the same overall dimensions. This table will probably be the only table you'll need if you have a small cabin. It can be used for food preparation, eating, playing board games and a general catchall. The stools provide very flexible seating and can be pushed under the table, completely out of the way, if more room is needed.

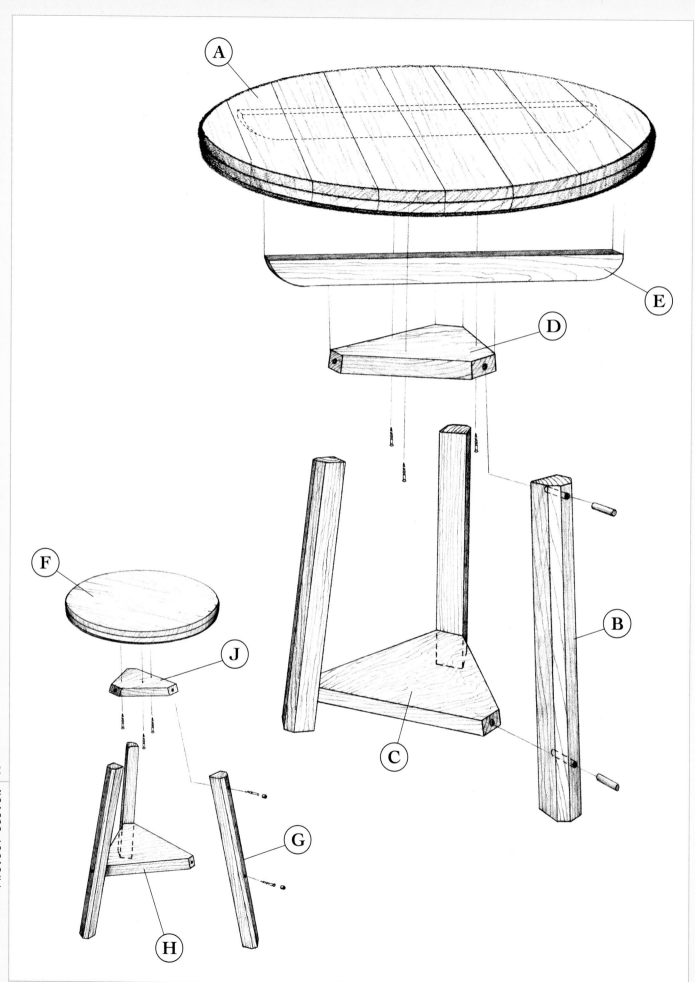

## MATERIALS LIST (INCHES) • DINING TABLE & STOOLS

| REF. | QTY. | PART | MATERIAL | THICKNESS | WIDTH | LENGTH | COMMENTS |
|------|------|------|----------|-----------|-------|--------|----------|
| **TABLE** | | | | | | | |
| A | 1 | Top | Sugar Pine | $1^{3}/_{8}$ | 40 dia. | | |
| B | 3 | Legs | Sugar Pine | $2^{3}/_{4}$ | $2^{3}/_{4}$ | 28 | w/ 7° angles on each end |
| C | 1 | Bottom Brace | Sugar Pine | $1^{1}/_{4}$ | $15^{1}/_{4}$ | $17^{5}/_{8}$ | w/ 7° angles at each clipped corner |
| D | 1 | Top Brace | Sugar Pine | $1^{1}/_{4}$ | $11^{1}/_{4}$ | $12^{3}/_{4}$ | w/ 7° angles at each clipped corner |
| E | 2 | Battens | Sugar Pine | $1^{1}/_{4}$ | 2 | 26 | w/ radius at each end |
| **STOOLS** | | | | | | | |
| F | 1 | Top | Sugar Pine | $1^{1}/_{4}$ | $13^{1}/_{2}$ dia. | | |
| G | 3 | Legs | Sugar Pine | $1^{1}/_{4}$ | $1^{1}/_{4}$ | $16^{3}/_{4}$ | w/ $13^{1}/_{2}$° angles on each end |
| H | 1 | Bottom Brace | Sugar Pine | 1 | 8 | $9^{1}/_{4}$ | w/ $13^{1}/_{2}$° angles at each clipped corner |
| J | 1 | Top Brace | Sugar Pine | 1 | $4^{1}/_{2}$ | $5^{1}/_{4}$ | w/ $13^{1}/_{2}$° angles at each clipped corner |

Note: Double-check the angle measurements on the table and the stools by drawing a full-scale elevation. This will save time and materials.

## MATERIALS LIST (MILLIMETERS) • DINING TABLE & STOOLS

| REF. | QTY. | PART | MATERIAL | THICKNESS | WIDTH | LENGTH | COMMENTS |
|------|------|------|----------|-----------|-------|--------|----------|
| **TABLE** | | | | | | | |
| A | 1 | Top | Sugar Pine | 35 | 1,000 dia. | | |
| B | 3 | Legs | Sugar Pine | 70 | 70 | 710 | w/ 7° angles on each end |
| C | 1 | Bottom Brace | Sugar Pine | 32 | 385 | 450 | w/ 7° angles at each clipped corner |
| D | 1 | Top Brace | Sugar Pine | 32 | 285 | 325 | w/ 7° angles at each clipped corner |
| E | 2 | Battens | Sugar Pine | 32 | 50 | 660 | w/ radius at each end |
| **STOOLS** | | | | | | | |
| F | 1 | Top | Sugar Pine | 32 | 345 dia. | | |
| G | 3 | Legs | Sugar Pine | 32 | 32 | 425 | w/ $13^{1}/_{2}$° angles on each end |
| H | 1 | Bottom Brace | Sugar Pine | 25 | 205 | 235 | w/ $13^{1}/_{2}$° angles at each clipped corner |
| J | 1 | Top Brace | Sugar Pine | 25 | 115 | 135 | w/ $13^{1}/_{2}$° angles at each clipped corner |

Note: Double-check the angle measurements on the table and the stools by drawing a full-scale elevation. This will save time and materials.

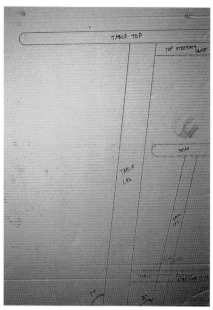

1 | It is recommended that a full-scale elevation of the table and stools be drawn so all angles may be accurately transferred to the parts.

2 | After cutting all the parts per the materials list, make a doweling jig. This jig will hold the drill bit at the proper angle when drilling the dowel holes for the table leg/stretcher panel joint. (See sidebar "Making a Homemade Doweling Jig" on page 14.)

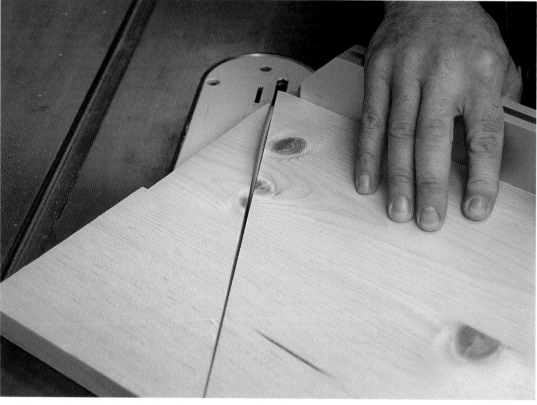

3 | Here you'll cut the triangle-shaped stretcher panel for the table and stool bases. After laying out the triangle to determine how large you need to make your stretcher panel blanks (see sidebar "Drawing an Equilateral Triangle"), glue up the blanks as squares, set the table saw miter gauge on 30° and make the first cut.

# DRAWING AN EQUILATERAL TRIANGLE

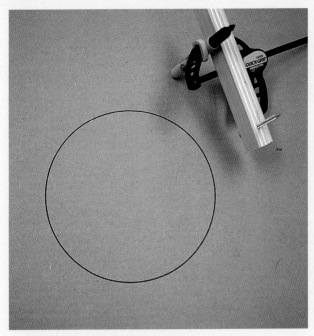

1 | First draw a circle with the diameter you've chosen.

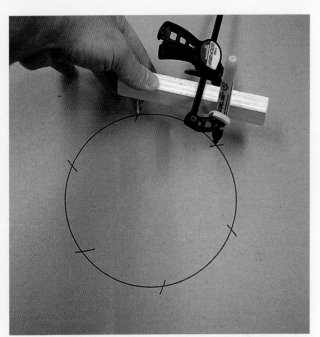

2 | Next, keeping the compass set to the radius, set the center on the circle line and strike a point on the circle. Continue doing this around the circle, dividing the circle into six equal sections.

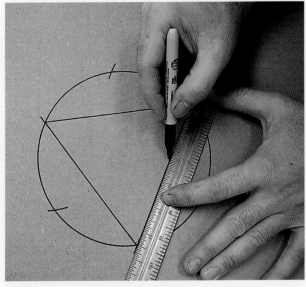

3 | Then connect every other point you drew on the circle.

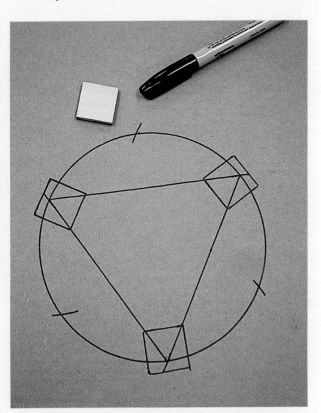

4 | Finally, determine the leg size and draw it at the triangle points. This will give you a full-size template for the connecting braces for the table and stools.

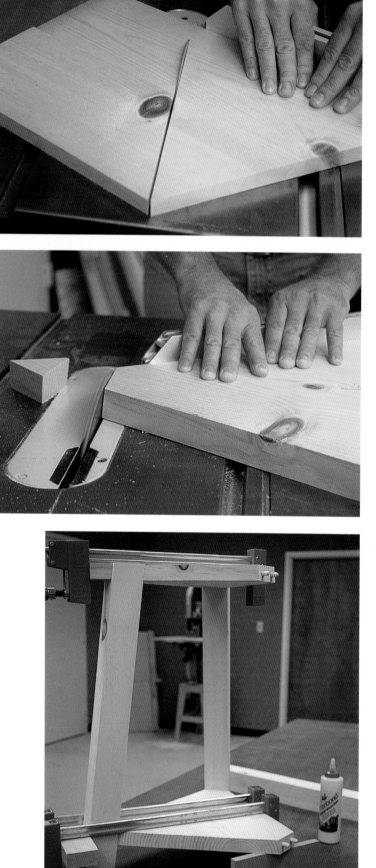

**4** Flip over the blank and make the second cut.

**5** To clip the ends of the triangle, reset the miter gauge to 30° on the other side of the gauge and set the blade to the required leg-splay angle. Hold the panel against the fence and cut off the end of the triangle. This creates the joint surface for the legs.

**6** Glue on one leg at a time. Note the use of angled clamp blocks. One clamp attaches to each side of the block. This evens out the clamping pressure applied to the leg/stretcher joint.

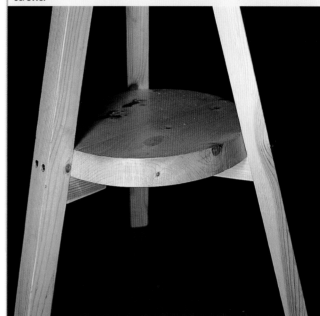

**TIP** *This is another method for making the table or stool base. Tilt your band saw table to the angle of leg splay and cut out a disc. Sand the edge and attach the legs with dowels or screws.*

**7** | Flip over the blank and make the second cut.

**8** | To soften the shape of the legs, rout a 45° angle on the two outside corners of the legs.

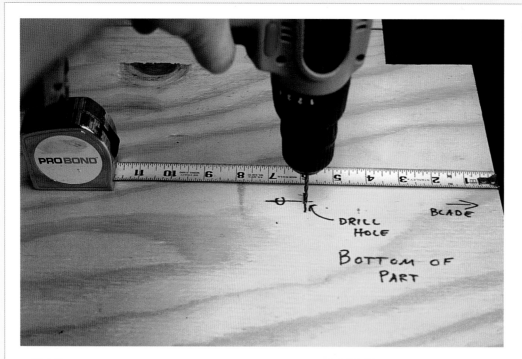

9 | It's easy to cut circles on the band saw. After the top and seat blanks have been glued up to size, mark a center on the blank and drill a hole at this mark on the bottom of the blank.

10 | This illustrates the proper setup of the circle-cutting jig on the band saw.

11 | Complete the circle cutout, and sand the edges of the top pieces. Rout a 45° bevel on the top and bottom edges.

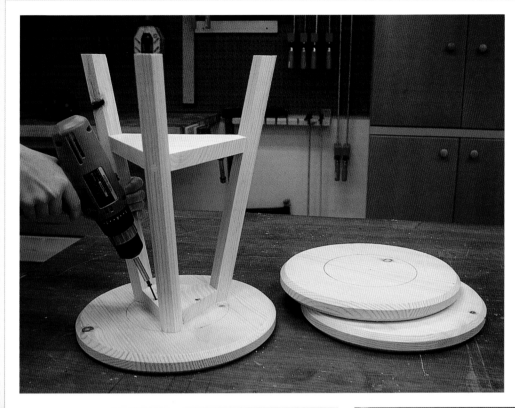

12 | Drill oversize holes in the top brace and attach the top (seat) pieces with screws. Do not use any glue.

13 | Cut out the two battens, round the ends and bevel the two long edges. Drill oversize holes in the battens and, using screws, attach them across the grain of the top. These battens will keep the top flat while allowing it to move according to changes in moisture. Again, do not use any glue.

14 | Stain the projects (if you choose) the color of your choice. Let the stain dry for half a day and apply the finish of your choice. These particular stools were stained dark and finished with three coats of pre-catalyzed lacquer.

# potting bench cabinet

CONSTRUCTION OF THIS CABINET IS fun. The process of texturing the wood surface adds to the appeal of the project. It has a variety of uses. Outside it can be used as a worktop for potting plants and storing gardening supplies. Indoors it can be used as a storage cabinet for dishes or books, or a great stand for a lamp or flower arrangement. And if the wood warps or twists, that will only add to the appeal of the piece!

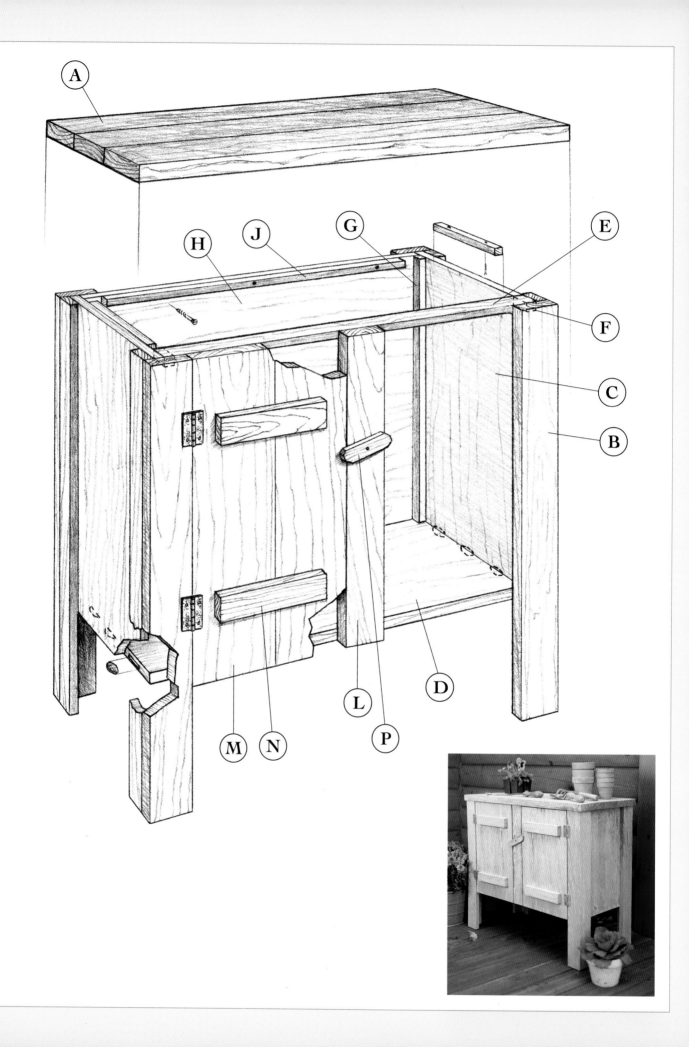

**MATERIALS LIST (INCHES)** • POTTING BENCH CABINET

| REF. | QTY. | PART | MATERIAL | THICKNESS | WIDTH | LENGTH | COMMENTS |
|---|---|---|---|---|---|---|---|
| A | 1 | Top | Yellow Pine | $1\frac{1}{4}$ | 16 | 34 | |
| B { | 4 | Legs | Yellow Pine | 3 | 3 | $28\frac{1}{2}$ | (see next two listed parts) |
| | 4 | Leg Panels | Yellow Pine | $\frac{3}{4}$ | $2\frac{1}{4}$ | $28\frac{1}{2}$ | |
| | 4 | Leg Panels | Yellow Pine | $\frac{3}{4}$ | 3 | $28\frac{1}{2}$ | |
| C | 2 | Side Panels | Yellow Pine | $\frac{7}{8}$ | $13\frac{3}{4}$ | $19\frac{3}{4}$ | |
| D | 1 | Bottom | Yellow Pine | 1 | $12\frac{7}{8}$ | $29\frac{3}{4}$ | |
| E | 1 | Top Rail | Yellow Pine | $\frac{3}{4}$ | 2 | $29\frac{3}{4}$ | |
| F | 2 | Blocks for Top Rail | Yellow Pine | $1\frac{3}{4}$ | 2 | $2\frac{3}{4}$ | |
| G | 2 | Cleats | Yellow Pine | $\frac{3}{4}$ | $\frac{3}{4}$ | 19 | |
| H | 1 | Back Panel | Yellow Pine | $\frac{7}{8}$ | $19\frac{3}{4}$ | $29\frac{3}{4}$ | |
| J | 1 | Cleat | Yellow Pine | $\frac{3}{4}$ | $\frac{3}{4}$ | $26\frac{1}{2}$ | |
| K | 2 | Cleats | Yellow Pine | $\frac{3}{4}$ | $\frac{3}{4}$ | 10 | |
| L | 1 | Front Stile | Yellow Pine | $\frac{7}{8}$ | $2\frac{1}{2}$ | $19\frac{3}{4}$ | |
| M | 2 | Doors | Yellow Pine | $\frac{7}{8}$ | $12\frac{1}{16}$ | $19\frac{5}{8}$ | |
| N | 4 | Battens | Yellow Pine | $\frac{3}{4}$ | $1\frac{3}{4}$ | 9 | |
| P | 1 | Flipper Door Latch | Yellow Pine | $\frac{1}{4}$ | $1\frac{1}{4}$ | $4\frac{1}{2}$ | |
| | 2 sets | $1\frac{1}{2}$" x 2" Rusted Hinges and Screws (see "Antiquing Hardware" on page 29) | | | | | |

**MATERIALS LIST (MILLIMETERS)** • POTTING BENCH CABINET

| REF. | QTY. | PART | MATERIAL | THICKNESS | WIDTH | LENGTH | COMMENTS |
|---|---|---|---|---|---|---|---|
| A | 1 | Top | Yellow Pine | 32 | 405 | 860 | |
| B { | 4 | Legs | Yellow Pine | 75 | 75 | 725 | (see next two listed parts) |
| | 4 | Leg Panels | Yellow Pine | 19 | 56 | 725 | |
| | 4 | Leg Panels | Yellow Pine | 19 | 75 | 725 | |
| C | 2 | Side Panels | Yellow Pine | 22 | 350 | 500 | |
| D | 1 | Bottom | Yellow Pine | 25 | 328 | 755 | |
| E | 1 | Top Rail | Yellow Pine | 19 | 50 | 755 | |
| F | 2 | Blocks for Top Rail | Yellow Pine | 45 | 50 | 75 | |
| G | 2 | Cleats | Yellow Pine | 19 | 19 | 480 | |
| H | 1 | Back Panel | Yellow Pine | 22 | 500 | 755 | |
| J | 1 | Cleat | Yellow Pine | 19 | 19 | 675 | |
| K | 2 | Cleats | Yellow Pine | 19 | 19 | 255 | |
| L | 1 | Front Stile | Yellow Pine | 22 | 65 | 500 | |
| M | 2 | Doors | Yellow Pine | 22 | 306 | 497.5 | |
| N | 4 | Battens | Yellow Pine | 19 | 45 | 230 | |
| P | 1 | Flipper Door Latch | Yellow Pine | 6 | 32 | 115 | |
| | 2 sets | 38mm x 50mm Rusted Hinges and Screws (see "Antiquing Hardware" on page 29) | | | | | |

1 Yellow pine is a softwood that has hard, fibrous growth rings. The soft wood between these rings can be removed with a wire brush mounted on an electric hand drill (as shown, above left). This creates a textured surface that appears to be weathered (above right).

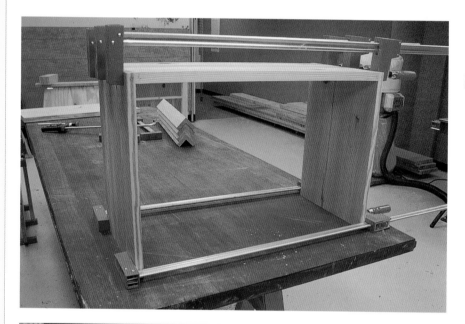

2 After all the outsides of the cabinet panels have been textured, the two end panels are glued to the bottom panel using biscuits. (Note the clamps resting on the assembly bench. These hold the assembly square while the glue cures.)

3 Install cleats on both sides. These will be used to attach the back panel to the cabinet.

4 | Drill ¼" holes for attaching the back to the cabinet. These oversize holes will allow the screws to move with the solid wood back.

5 | Using biscuits and glue, attach the back panel to the bottom panel.

6 | Use screws through the cleats to attach the back panel to the sides.

7 | Cut the leg parts to size, texture them on one side and one long edge. Glue up four right-angle assemblies. Double-check for squareness.

8 | Install the rail mounting blocks, and attach the top front rail to the blocks. Then attach the legs to the cabinet with screws from the inside of the cabinet. Keep the legs flush with the top of the cabinet. Using biscuits and glue, attach the front divider to the top rail and bottom panel.

9 | Cut the two doors to size and double-check that they fit on the cabinet. Texture them and the four front battens. Attach the battens to the doors with screws. Again, drill ¼" (6mm) oversize holes so the screws will move with the door panels. The battens help to keep the doors flat and work great as handles.

10 | Use a light brown stain to enhance the textured soft grain. (The soft grain will absorb the stain very easily.) When the stain dries, seal it with one coat of finish.

11 | When the finish dries, apply a white stain to the wood. Wipe off the excess stain and the rest of it will stay in the deeper parts of the texturing. After the stain dries (about 4 hours), apply two top coats of finish. This project was finished with two top coats of satin sheen pre-catalyzed lacquer.

12 | Lay the cabinet on its back to install the doors. The rusted hinges can then be mounted on the faces of the cabinet and the doors. The door latch is screwed into place just tight enough to keep it from spinning freely.

# laced bentwood rocker

WHEN ALL THE WORK IS DONE (IS IT ever?), this is the chair you will choose to relax, and probably doze off, in. The lacing is a very important part of this chair, as it provides the sitting and leaning parts. The lacing is tight, flexible, incredibly strong, and will "give" in the right places when you sit down. Ash by nature is very strong, springy and easily bent, which adds to the overall comfort. You will be rewarded ten times over for the work involved in making this chair. So get up and start building. You'll be able to sit down and rock that much sooner.

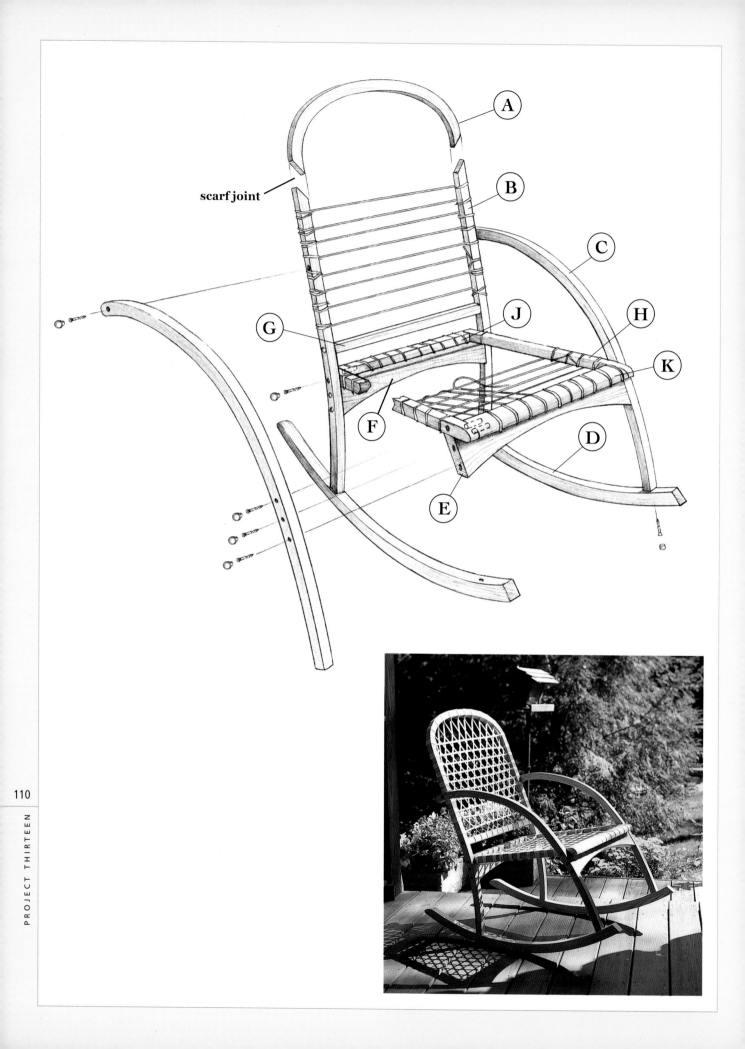

scarf joint

A

B

C

G

J

H

K

F

D

E

## MATERIALS LIST (INCHES) • LACED BENTWOOD ROCKER

| REF. | QTY. | PART | MATERIAL | THICKNESS | WIDTH | LENGTH | COMMENTS |
|------|------|------|----------|-----------|-------|--------|----------|
| A | 1 | *Crest Rail | Ash | $1^{1}/_{8}$ | $1^{1}/_{8}$ | $22^{1}/_{4}$ | |
| B | 2 | *Back Legs | Ash | $1^{1}/_{8}$ | $1^{1}/_{8}$ | 30 | |
| C | 2 | *Arms | Ash | $1^{1}/_{8}$ | $1^{1}/_{8}$ | $34^{1}/_{2}$ | |
| D | 2 | *Rockers | Ash | $1^{1}/_{4}$ | $1^{1}/_{2}$ | $37^{1}/_{2}$ | |
| E | 1 | Front Rail | Ash | 1 | 3 | $21^{7}/_{8}$ | |
| F | 1 | Back Rail | Ash | 1 | 3 | 20 | |
| G | 1 | Back Lacing Rail | Ash | $1^{1}/_{8}$ | $1^{1}/_{8}$ | 20 | |
| H | 2 | Side Seat Rails | Ash | $1^{1}/_{8}$ | $1^{1}/_{8}$ | 22 | |
| J | 1 | Back Seat Rail | Ash | $1^{1}/_{8}$ | $1^{1}/_{8}$ | $17^{5}/_{8}$ | $3^{1}/_{2}°$ angles on each end |
| K | 1 | Front Seat Rail | Ash | $1^{1}/_{8}$ | 2 | $19^{3}/_{4}$ | $3^{1}/_{2}°$ angles on each end |
| | 14 | $^{3}/_{8}$" mushroom buttons | Birch | | | | |
| | 2 | $^{1}/_{2}$" mushroom buttons | Birch | | | | |

*Note: All laminated parts are made of $^{1}/_{8}$"-thick pieces. Add 8" to 10" to the rough stock lengths when cutting. This will allow plenty of material to make the bends. These laminated parts can then be easily cut to the proper lengths.

*Note: It is recommended that the builder draw full-scale side and front elevations to determine the exact lengths and angles of all parts.

## MATERIALS LIST (MILLIMETERS) • LACED BENTWOOD ROCKER

| REF. | QTY. | PART | MATERIAL | THICKNESS | WIDTH | LENGTH | COMMENTS |
|------|------|------|----------|-----------|-------|--------|----------|
| A | 1 | *Crest Rail | Ash | 30 | 30 | 565 | |
| B | 2 | *Back Legs | Ash | 30 | 30 | 760 | |
| C | 2 | *Arms | Ash | 30 | 30 | 875 | |
| D | 2 | *Rockers | Ash | 33 | 38 | 950 | |
| E | 1 | Front Rail | Ash | 25 | 75 | 556 | |
| F | 1 | Back Rail | Ash | 25 | 75 | 508 | |
| G | 1 | Back Lacing Rail | Ash | 30 | 30 | 508 | |
| H | 2 | Side Seat Rails | Ash | 30 | 30 | 559 | |
| J | 1 | Back Seat Rail | Ash | 30 | 30 | 448 | $3^{1}/_{2}°$ angles on each end |
| K | 1 | Front Seat Rail | Ash | 30 | 50 | 502 | $3^{1}/_{2}°$ angles on each end |
| | 14 | 9.5mm mushroom buttons | Birch | | | | |
| | 2 | 12.5mm mushroom buttons | Birch | | | | |

*Note: All laminated parts are made of 5mm-thick pieces. Add 200mm to 250mm to the rough stock lengths when cutting. This will allow plenty of material to make the bends. These laminated parts can then be easily cut to the proper lengths.

*Note: It is recommended that the builder draw full-scale side and front elevations to determine the exact lengths and angles of all parts.

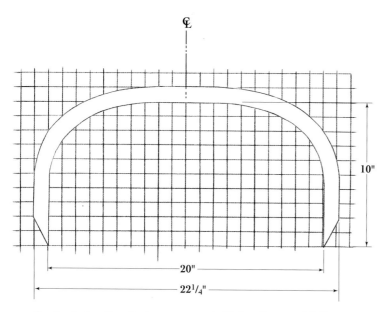

10"

20"

22¹/₄"

Crest rail elevation. Each square equals 1". See the materials list for millimeter conversions.

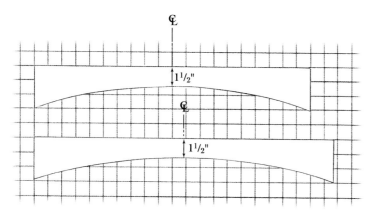

1¹/₂"

1¹/₂"

Front and back rail elevations.

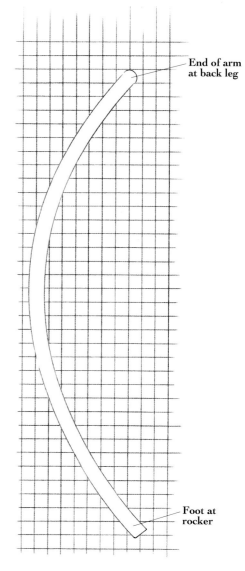

**End of arm at back leg**

**Foot at rocker**

Rocker elevation.

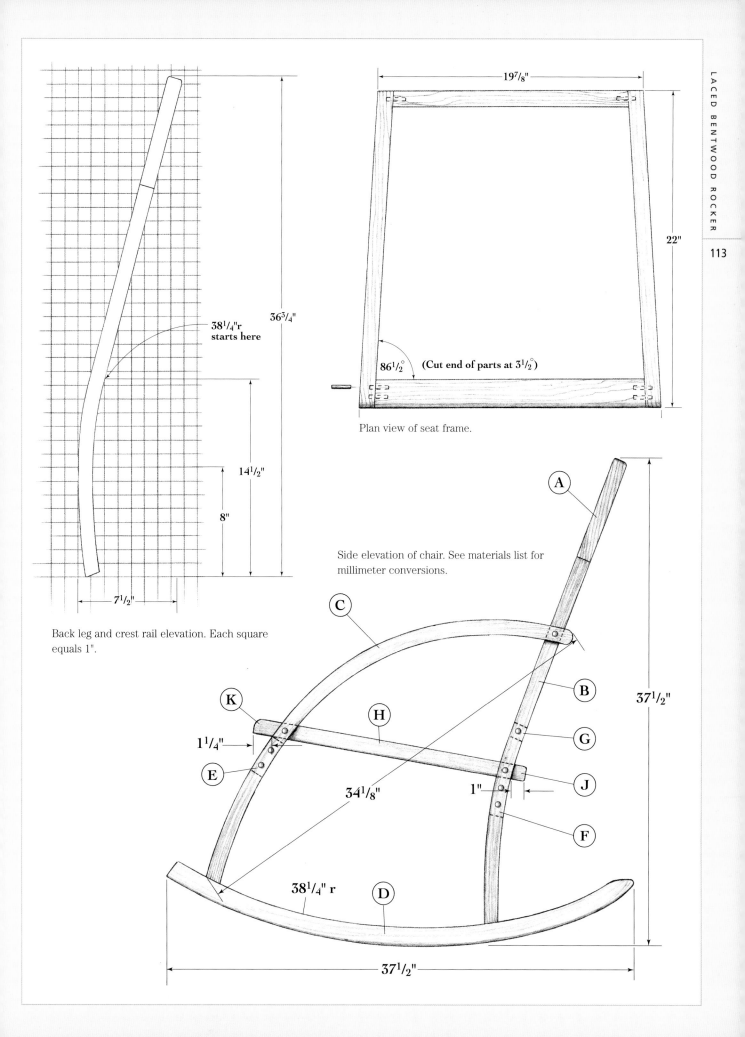

19⁷/₈"

22"

**(Cut end of parts at 3¹/₂°)**

86¹/₂°

Plan view of seat frame.

38¹/₄"r
starts here

36³/₄"

14¹/₂"

8"

7¹/₂"

Back leg and crest rail elevation. Each square
equals 1".

Side elevation of chair. See materials list for
millimeter conversions.

A

C

K

1¹/₄"

E

B

H

G

J

1"

F

34¹/₈"

37¹/₂"

38¹/₄" r

D

37¹/₂"

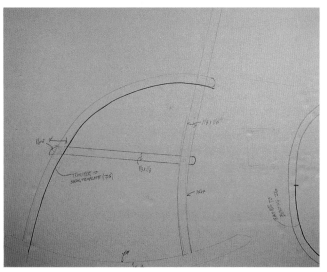

1 | Draw a full-scale elevation so that you can size all parts directly from the drawing. The elevation also provides the pattern for the bending jigs that you will need. Trace the shapes for each of the bending jigs and transfer them to the stock for the jigs. (It is recommended that two layers of ¾" {19mm} medium-density fiberboard [MDF] be used to make the jigs.) Cut out the patterns, and sand the lines smooth so they flow nicely.

2 | Mill the stock for all of the bent parts to 1⅛" (3mm) thickness and mark the stock face with the orientation triangle. Slice the parts on the band saw and keep them in order as they are cut. If you have access to a thickness planer or a thickness sander, mill all the strips to a ⅛" thickness. (The strips can be used just as they come off the band saw. The saw cuts may create some gaps at glue-up.)

3 | Lay out all the laminations in order of assembly and apply yellow wood glue with a small paint roller. This is a very quick and tidy way to get all the laminations coated with glue. As each piece is coated, put it on top of the preceding piece. Then take this assembly to the gluing jig.

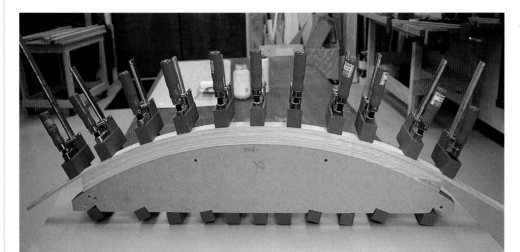

**4** Clamp the rocker. Note the longer extra strip. This prevents the rocker from being dented by the clamps and also distributes the clamping pressure more evenly.

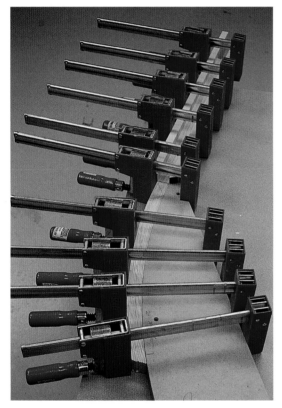

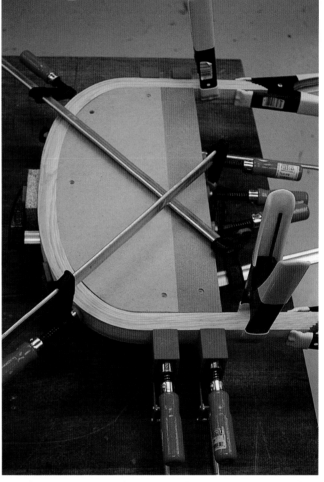

**5** About one-third of the jig used to glue up the rockers is used to glue up the back legs. (The bottom part of each leg has the same radius as the rockers.) The upper part of each leg is sandwiched between two straight gluing cauls.

**6** Glue up the crest rail. At the bends, don't try to clamp with too much pressure. The bend will smooth itself out nicely if it isn't forced. Use just enough clamping pressure to close the laminations tightly. When doing a bend like this, start clamping in the center of the piece and work your way out evenly in both directions. You might need an assistant to help with this glue-up.

8 | Cutting the ends of the crest rail to length makes it easier to lay out where you will make the scarf joint cuts. Using the fence and miter gauge together is an easy and safe operation.

7 | When all the laminations have been done, clean them up with a hand plane or on the jointer. Then plane them to the desired thickness on a thickness planer. If you don't have access to a planer, cut the pieces to thickness on the table saw as shown. Then plane or sand the saw marks until smooth.

9 | Cut the back leg to length. Hold the straight part of the leg against the miter gauge fence and determine the angle needed to make the cut. (The cut line is determined by referring to the full-scale drawings.)

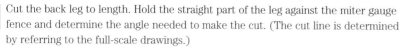

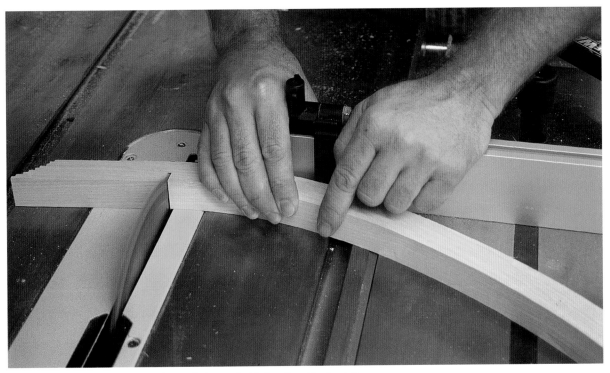

**10** Put a spacer behind the rocker to help you hold the piece firmly at the proper angle. Here, the adjustable stop is being used as a spacer.

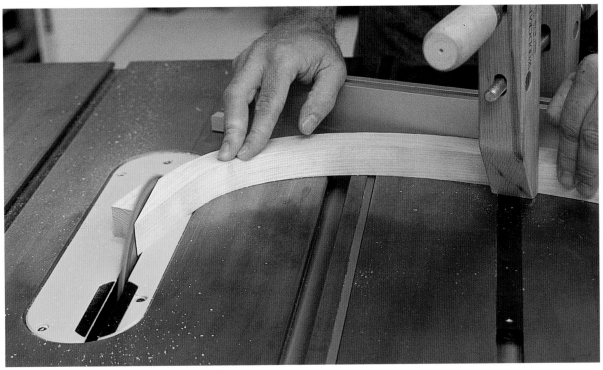

**11** After determining the location of the scarf joint from the full-scale drawings, transfer the cutting line to the crest rail. Use the cutting line as a guide for lining up the piece to make the cut. Clamp the crest rail to the miter gauge when you make the cut.

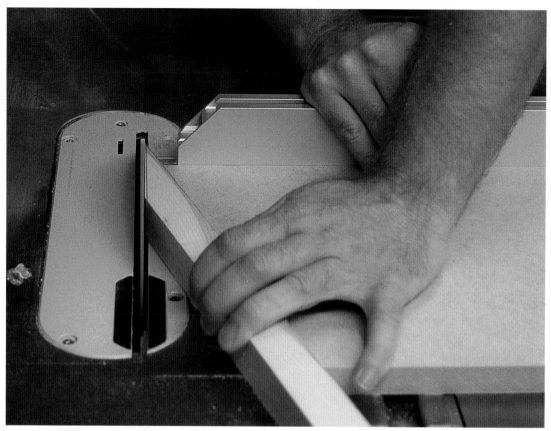

**12** Cut the scarf joint on the back leg. This is a very steep cut. After making the jig shown, this cut is easily done. Put some sandpaper on the edge of the jig where the leg will be held against it. This will help prevent the leg from slipping when you are making the cut. Also, don't try to cut through all the material at one time. Nibble your way to the cut line. This helps control the piece being cut. (If you feel uncomfortable making this cut on the table saw, use a band saw to make the cut and then sand or plane the angle until smooth.)

**13** Dry fit the scarf joint before gluing. When the joint is correct, use a caul to hold the pieces in alignment, glue and clamp. Because of the large gluing surface of this joint, it is very strong.

**14** After the front and back rails are cut out and trimmed to length, do a dry fit of the chair. This will help you see how it all goes together.

**15** Using a homemade doweling jig (see page 14) that has been cut on an angle, drill the holes for the dowels in the seat parts.

16 | After the seat parts have been assembled, shape the front of the seat to a roundover that is pleasing to your eye and touch. When all the chair parts have been dry assembled and it all looks good, disassemble the parts and sand them, working your way to at least 150-grit sandpaper. Then finish all the parts while they are apart. This project was finished with three coats of satin sheen pre-catalyzed lacquer.

## LACING THE ROCKER

After you have finished the chair parts, now it is time to do the lacing. The lacing materials are sold as a kit, and the cost is extremely reasonable. Because the lacing could be a chapter all by itself, I highly recommend contacting Country Ways (see below) for all the necessary materials and detailed instruction for the lacing.

Country Ways
6001 Lyndale Ave. S.
Minneapolis, MN 55419
(800) 216-0710
www.snowshoe.com

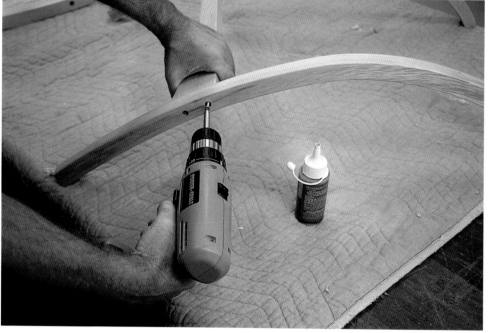

17 | When the chair parts have been finished and the seat and back assemblies have been laced, the chair can be assembled. Drill and countersink the holes for the screws. Put a couple of drops of polyurethane glue on the screws to help them stay tight.

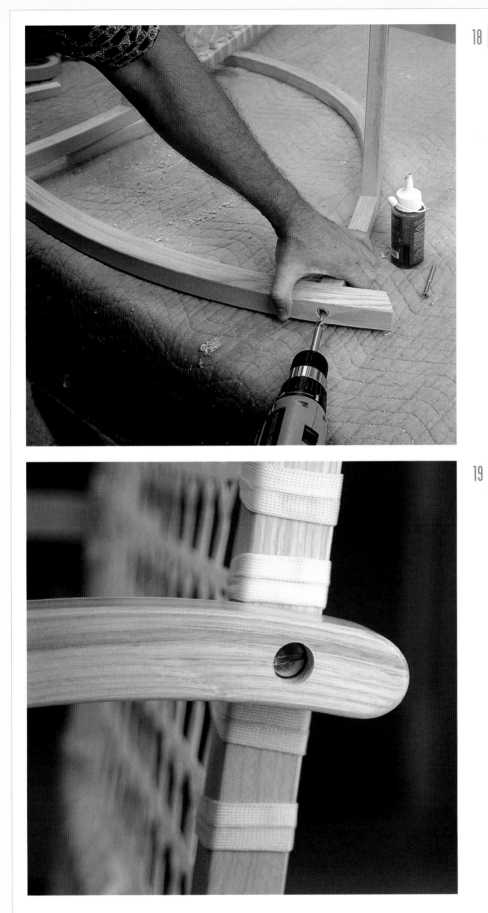

18 | Use No. 12 × 3" (75mm) flathead sheet metal screws to attach the rockers to the legs. Again, put some polyurethane glue on the screws.

19 | This detail shows the front leg/arm and back leg joint. The arm joins the back leg between the lacing wraps.

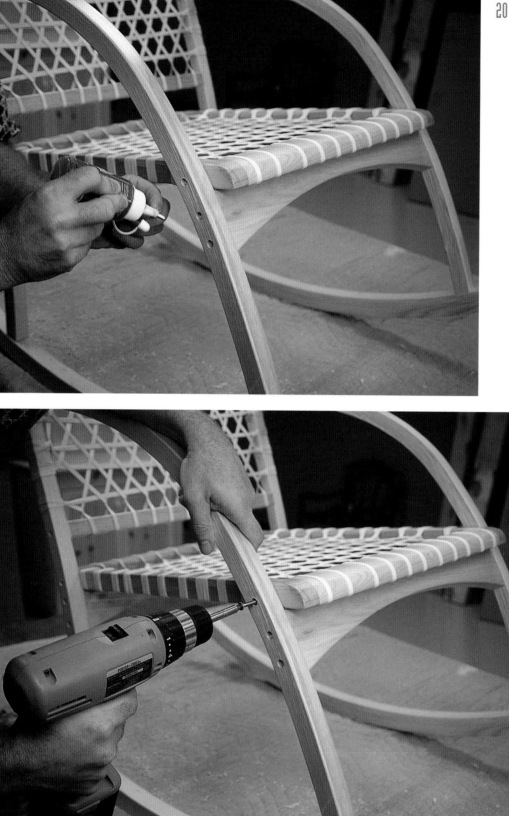

**21** Then drive the screw home. Note the counterbored holes for the mushroom plugs.

# DETAILS OF THE ROCKER

Mushroom plugs glued in place.

Front of the detail. The rockers angle toward each other at the back of the chair. When you rock back in the chair, this angling causes the chair to rock forward. You only have to push back again. And so it goes!

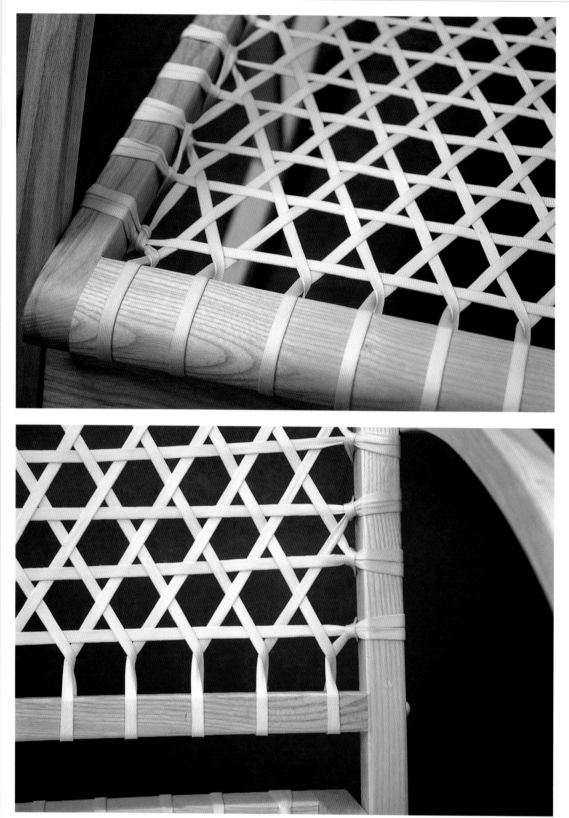

Detail of seat lacing.

Detail of back lacing.

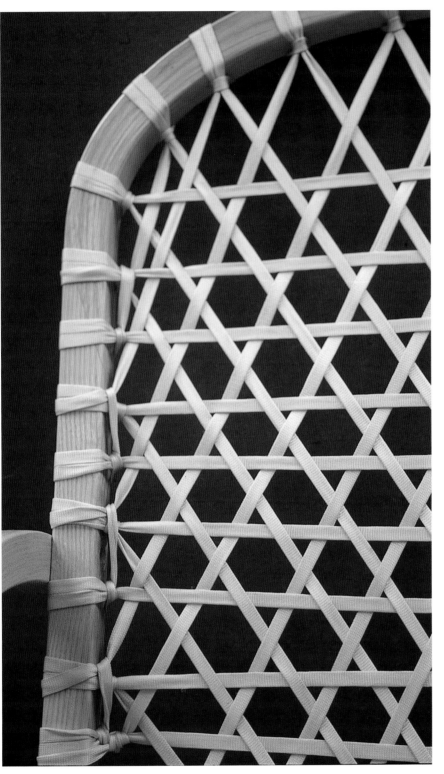

Detail of lacing at
the crest rail.

# index

# COMMON WOODWORKING TERMS

**BEVEL** A cut that is not 90° to a board's face, or the facet left by such a cut.

**BISCUIT** A thin, flat oval of compressed beechwood that is inserted between two pieces of wood into mating saw kerfs made by a biscuit joiner.

**BRIDLE JOINT** A joint that combines features of both lap joints and mortise and tenon. It has a U-shaped mortise in the end of the board.

**BUTT JOINT** Two flat facets of mating parts that fit flush together with no interlocking joinery.

**CARPENTER'S GLUE** White and yellow adhesives formulated for use with wood.

**CASING** The trim framing a window, door or other opening.

**CHALK LINE** Line made by snapping a chalk-coated string against a plane.

**CHECK** A crack in wood material caused by drying, either in the surface or in the ends of the board so the fibers have separated.

**COMPOUND MITER** A cut where the blade path is not perpendicular to the wood's end or edge and the blade tilt is not 90° to the face.

**COPING** Sawing a negative profile in one piece to fit the positive profile of another, usually in moulding.

**COUNTERBORE** A straight-sided drilled hole that recesses a screw head below the wood surface so a wood plug can cover it, or the bit which makes this hole.

**COUNTERSINK** A cone-shaped drilled hole whose slope angle matches the underside of a flat screw head and sinks it flush with the wood surface; or the tool which makes this hole.

**CROSSCUT** To saw wood perpendicular to the grain.

**CUPPING** A drying defect in which one side of the board shrinks more across the grain than the other, causing the board to curl in on itself like a trough.

**DADO** A flat-bottomed, U-shaped milling cut of varying widths and depths but always running across the grain.

**DOVETAIL JOINT** A traditional joint characterized by interlocking fingers and pockets shaped like its name. It has exceptional resistance to tension.

**DOWEL** A small cylinder of wood that is used to reinforce a wood joint.

**DRESSING** The process of turning rough lumber into a smooth board with flat, parallel faces and straight, parallel edges and whose edges are square to the face.

**EDGE LAP** A notch into the edge of a board halfway across its width which forms half of an edge lap joint.

**FINGERLAP** A specific joint of the lap family which has straight, interwoven fingers; also called a box joint.

**FINISH** Varnish, stain, paint, or any mixture that protects a surface.

**FLATSAWN** The most common cut of lumber where the growth rings run predominantly across the end of the board; or its characteristic grain pattern.

**FLUSH** Level with an adjoining surface.

**GRAIN PATTERN** The visual appearance of wood grain. Types of grain pattern include flat, straight, curly, quilted, rowed, mottled, crotch, cathedral, beeswing or bird's-eye.

**HARDWOOD** Wood from broadleaf deciduous trees, no matter what the density (balsa is a hardwood).

**HEARTWOOD** Wood from the core of a tree, usually darker and harder than newer wood.

**JIG** A shop-made or aftermarket device that assists in positioning and steadying the wood or tools.

**JOINTING** The process of making a board face straight and flat, or an edge straight, whether by hand or machine.

**KERF** The visible path of subtracted wood left by a sawblade.

**KEY** An inserted joint-locking device, usually made of wood.

**KNOCKDOWN JOINT** A joint which is assembled without glue and can be disassembled and reassembled if necessary.

**LAP JOINT** A type of joint made by removing half the thickness or width of the parts and lapping them over each other.

**LENGTH JOINT** A joint which makes one longer wood unit out of two shorter ones by joining them end to end.

**LEVEL** Absolutely horizontal.

**MILLING** The process of removing material to leave a desired positive or negative profile in the wood.

**MITER** A generic term meaning mainly an angled cut across the face grain, or specifically 45° cut across the face, end grain, or along the grain. *See also* bevel.

**MORTISE** The commonly rectangular or round pocket into which a mating tenon is inserted. Mortises can be blind (stop inside the wood thickness), through, or open on one end.

**PARTICLEBOARD** A panel made of wood particles and glue.

**PILOT HOLE** A small, drilled hole used as a guide and pressure relief for screw insertion, or to locate additional drilling work like countersinking and counterboring.

**PLYWOOD** Panel made by laminating layers of wood.

**QUARTERSAWN** A stable lumber cut where the growth rings on the board's end run more vertically across the end than horizontal and the grain on the face looks straight; also called straight-grained or riftsawn.

**RABBET** A milled cut which leaves a flat step parallel to, but recessed from, the wood's surface.

**RAIL** The name of the horizontal parts of a door frame.

**RIP** To cut parallel to the grain of a board.

**SAPWOOD** The new wood in a tree, located between the core (heartwood) and bark. Usually lighter in color.

**SCARF JOINT** A joint that increases the overall length of wood by joining two pieces at their ends, commonly by gluing together two unusually long bevels in their faces or edges.

**SCRIBE** To make layout lines or index marks using a knife or awl.

**SHOULDER** The perpendicular face of a step cut like a rabbet which bears against a mating joint part to stabilize the joint.

**SOFTWOOD** Wood from coniferous evergreen trees, no matter what the density (yew is a softwood).

**SPLINE** A flat, thin strip of wood that fits into mating grooves between two parts to reinforce the joint between them.

**STAIN** A pigment or dye used to color wood through saturation, or, a discoloration in wood from fungus or chemicals.

**STILE** The name of the vertical parts of a door frame.

**TENON** The male part of a mortise-and-tenon joint, commonly rectangular or round, but not restricted to those shapes.

**TONGUE AND GROOVE** Joinery method in which one board is cut with a protruding groove and another is cut with a matching groove along its edge.

**TWISTING** A drying defect in lumber that causes it to twist so the faces at the end of the board are in a different plane.

**VENEER** A thin sheet of wood bonded to another material.

**WIDTH JOINT** A joint which makes a unit of the parts by joining them edge to edge to increase the overall width of wood.

# More of the best from
## *Popular Woodworking Books*

**Build Your Own Home Office Furniture**
With designs ranging from weekend projects to a fully realized computer desk, all of the plans in this book are fresh, functional and fun to build. Easy-to-follow instructions accompany detailed photographs that show all the key steps. #70489/$26.99/128 pages/300 color illus./paperback

**How to Build Classic Garden Furniture**
This easy, step-by-step guide will have you anxious to begin crafting this elegant outdoor furniture. The 20 projects included are designed to withstand years of outdoor exposure with minimal care, and are versatile enough to complement any home's style. Each beautiful piece is easy to tackle with full-color illustrations, numbered steps, close-up photos as well as alternatives for design, wood selection and finishing. #70395/$24.99/128 pages/275 color, 69 b&w illus./paperback

**Quick & Easy Furniture You Can Build with Dimensional Lumber**
This book ensures that you get the most for your money when it comes to purchasing and building with framing lumber. It covers every aspect of the furniture-making process with step-by-step instructions, precise measurements, full-color photos, tips and sidebars. #70459/$22.99/128 pages/250 color images/paperback

**Authentic Arts & Crafts Furniture Projects**
Whatever your skill level, you'll find something special in this beautifully crafted book. Each classic furniture project is taken from the files of Popular Woodworking, the skill-building project magazine for practical woodworkers. #70499/$24.99/128 pages/200 color images/paperback

**Making Elegant Custom Tables**
Author Doug Stove elevates building tables to a fine art as you are guided through the process of crafting beautiful custom tables through nine different projects, explored in magnificent full-color photographs and 3-D illustrations. You'll find all the key techniques you need to make practical, yet exquisite, tables. #70493/$24.99/128 pages/200 color illus./paperback

**Classic Country Furniture**
Packed with 20 attractive and functional projects, this guide provides you with the perfect mix of techniques, woods and designs for building country furniture. Fully illustrated steps and instructions accompany each piece, so you can complete projects without any guesswork. #70475/$19.99/128 pages/250 color images/paperback

**Smart Shelving & Storage Solutions**
These innovative and inexpensive storage solutions are perfect for do-it-yourselfers. From bookshelves, chests and cabinets, to armoires, closet systems and benches, you'll find more than 27 woodworking projects to help you make the most of your space – whether it's under the bed, over the sink or in the garage. #70445/$24.99/144 pages/360 color, 40 b&w illus./paperback

**The Weekend Woodworker**
A fantastic resource for the straightforward, step-by-step projects you like! This book offers you a range of attractive challenges, from smaller items – such as a stylish CD rack, mailbox or birdhouse – to larger, easy-to-assemble projects, including a wall cupboard, child's bed, computer workstation or coffee table. Each project provides clear and easy step-by-step instructions, photographs and diagrams, ideal for both the beginner and expert. #70456/$22.99/144 pages/200 color photos/paperback

**25 Essential Projects for Your Workshop**
This collection contains some of the most popular projects from Popular Woodworking magazine! Each one has been designed for practical use in the woodshop – clever stands, cabinets, storage devices and more. In addition, helpful "shop tips" are sprinkled throughout each chapter, providing invaluable insight and advice. #70472/$22.99/128 pages/275 color images/paperback